SCHOLASTIC
LITERACY SKILLS

Vocabulary
Year 3

Author
Sue Taylor

Development editor
Rachel Mackinnon

Copy editor
Sarah Sodhi

Assistant editors
Helen Dawes and Jenny Regan

**CD-ROM design and
development team**
Joy Monkhouse, Anna Oliwa,
Micky Pledge, Rebecca Male,
Allison Parry, James Courier,
Jim Peacock/Beehive Illustration

Series designers
Shelley Best and Anna Oliwa

Book layout
Quadrum Solutions Ltd

Illustrations
Woody Fox

Designed using Adobe Indesign
Published by Scholastic Ltd, Book End,
Range Road, Witney,
Oxfordshire OX29 0YD
www.scholastic.co.uk

Printed by Bell & Bain Ltd, Glasgow
Text © 2010 Sue Taylor
© 2010 Scholastic Ltd
1 2 3 4 5 6 7 8 9 0   0 1 2 3 4 5 6 7 8 9

British Library Cataloguing-in-Publication Data
A catalogue record for this book is available from
the British Library.
ISBN 978-1407-10224-5

Mixed Sources
Product group from well-managed
forests and other controlled sources
www.fsc.org Cert no. TT-COC-002769
© 1996 Forest Stewardship Council

Acknowledgements

The publishers gratefully acknowledge permission to reproduce
the following copyright material:

Allan Ahlberg for the use of 'Things I have been doing lately' by
Allan Ahlberg from *Heard it in the playground* by Allan Ahlberg
© 1991, Allan Ahlberg (1991, Puffin). **John Foster** for the use of
'Where the wind blows' by John Foster from *Four O'Clock Friday*
by John Foster © 1991, John Foster (1991, Oxford University Press).
The Maggie Noach Literary Agency for the use of an extract
from *Skellig* by David Almond © 1998, David Almond (1998,
Hodder Children's Books). **Penguin Group** for the print use of
an extract from *Charlotte's Web* by E B White © 1952, E B White
(1952, Hamish Hamilton). **United Agents** for the use of the poem
'On and on' by Roger McGough from *Lucky* by Roger McGough
© 1993, Roger McGough (1993, Viking). **Celia Warren** for the
use of 'Squirrel' by Celia Warren from *The Works* chosen by Paul
Cookson © 2000, Celia Warren (2000, Macmillan).

Every effort has been made to trace copyright holders for the
works reproduced in this book, and the publishers apologise for
any inadvertent omissions.

Extracts from Primary National Strategy's Primary Framework for
Literacy (2006) http://nationalstrategies.standards.dcsf.gov.uk/
primary/primaryframework/ © Crown copyright. Reproduced under
the terms of the Click Use Licence.

Due to the nature of the web, we cannot guarantee the content or
links of any site mentioned. We strongly recommend that teachers
check websites before using them in the classroom.

Contents

Chapter 1
Synonyms and antonyms

Chapter 2
Word families, roots and meanings

Chapter 3
Grammar

Chapter 4
Cross-curricular vocabulary

Chapter 5
Fun with words

Introduction

Scholastic Literacy Skills: Vocabulary series

By Year 3 the majority of children are able to decode effectively for reading and have a developing bank of words that they recognise on sight. However, readers must know what most of the words mean before they can understand what they are reading. If a word is decoded accurately, but without meaning, comprehension is limited. Readers use their oral vocabulary to make sense of words they see in print. Children with more limited vocabulary are less likely to understand what they hear and what they read, and to access discussion, instructions and the curriculum itself. They are equally less likely to express themselves effectively in speaking and in writing.

This book provides a bank of adaptable ideas and resources for teaching vocabulary, both receptive vocabulary (word meanings recognised in context), and expressive vocabulary (word meanings known well enough that they can be used appropriately) in a wide range of contexts, both oral and written. The activities arise from or make links to different types of texts and to different curriculum areas. It is anticipated that activities will be selected to fit in with medium-term planning.

Teaching vocabulary

We learn words through many exposures to examples in context, both spoken and written. Vocabulary can be developed indirectly, when children engage daily in oral language, listen to adults read to them and read extensively on their own. Vocabulary should also, however, be taught directly, both as individual words and word-learning strategies. Children crucially need to develop an interest in and curiosity about words and meanings. Good vocabulary teaching involves active engagement and fosters excitement about words, which leads to children attending more closely to them. Model the use of significant and interesting vocabulary often and in different contexts. Develop a habit and culture in the class of seeking out and exploring new words. Celebrate original and exciting uses of vocabulary with rewards and through display. Have fun with games, jokes and word play, puns and double meanings. Above all, children need rich oral and written language experiences to see that words are important, interesting and fun.

About the product

This book contains five chapters of activities for teaching vocabulary. Each chapter focuses on a different vocabulary area, and is organised into four sections with clear objectives, background information for the concepts taught, teaching ideas, and photocopiable pages for use in whole-class teaching, with groups or for independent work. Each chapter also has a poster, assessment, Word of the week section and Fun with words sections. The word bank at the end of the book provides banks of words to be used in games and other activities linked to this book.

Posters

Each chapter has one poster. These posters are related to the subject of the chapter and should be displayed and used for reference throughout the work on the chapter. The poster notes (on the chapter introduction page) offer suggestions for how they could be used. There are black and white versions in the book and full-colour versions on the CD-ROM for you to print out or display on your whiteboard.

Assessment

Each chapter has an assessment section. It summarises the objectives and activities in the section, provides pointers on observation and record keeping and includes one assessment photocopiable page (which is also printable from the CD-ROM with answers, where appropriate).

Word of the week and Fun with words

For each chapter there are notes on Word of the week and Fun with words. Word of the week provides one word you might like to focus on related to each section. Fun with words provides general activities to use with your class throughout work on the chapter.

Word bank

The word bank at the end of each book provides a list of words you might like to use in games or other activities.

Activities

Each section contains three activities. These activities all take the form of a photocopiable page which is in the book.

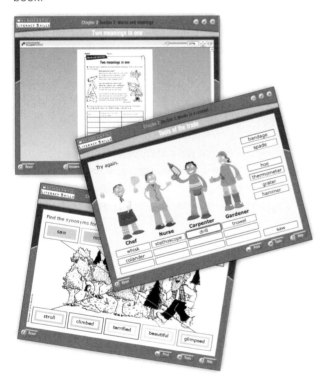

Each photocopiable page is also included on the CD-ROM for you to display or print out (these pages are also provided with answers where appropriate). Many of the photocopiable pages have linked interactive activities on the CD-ROM. These interactive activities are designed to act as starter activities to the lesson, giving whole-class support on the information being taught. However, they can work equally well as plenary activities, reviewing the work the children have just completed.

Differentiation

Activities in this book are not differentiated explicitly, although teacher notes may make suggestions for support or extension. Many of the activities can be used with the whole class with extra support provided through differentiated and open-ended questions, use of additional adults, mixed-ability paired or group work or additional input and consolidation before and/or after lessons. Some children may need support with the reading aspects of tasks in order to participate in the vocabulary objectives.

Using the CD-ROM

Below are brief guidance notes for using the CD-ROM. For more detailed information, see **How to use** on the start-up screen, or **Help** on the relevant screen for information about that page.

The CD-ROM follows the structure of the book and contains:
- All of the photocopiable pages.
- All of the poster pages in full colour.
- Photocopiable pages (with answers where appropriate).
- Thirty interactive on-screen activities linked to the photocopiable pages.

Getting started

To begin using the CD-ROM, simply place it in your CD- or DVD-ROM drive. Although the CD-ROM should auto-run, if it fails to do so, navigate to the drive and double-click on the red **Start** icon.

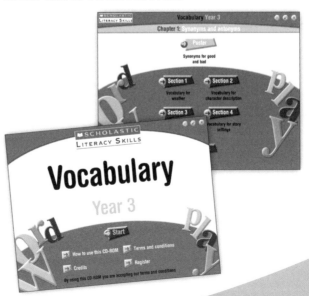

Start-up screen

The start-up screen is the first screen that appears. Here you can access: terms and conditions, registration links, how to use the CD-ROM and credits. If you agree to the terms and conditions, click **Start** to continue.

Main menu

The main menu provides links to all of the chapters or all of the resources. Clicking on the relevant **Chapter** icon will take you to the chapter screen where you can access the posters and the chapter's sections. Clicking on **All resources** will take you to a list of all the resources, where you can search by key word or chapter for a specific resource.

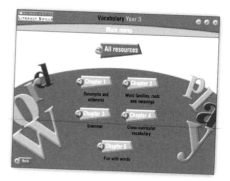

Section screen

Upon choosing a section from the chapter screen, you are taken to a list of resources for that section. Here you can access all of the photocopiable pages related to that section as well as the linked interactive activities.

Resource finder

The **Resource finder** lists all of the resources on the CD-ROM. You can:

- Select a chapter and/or section by selecting the appropriate title from the drop-down menus.
- Search for key words by typing them into the search box.
- Scroll up or down the list of resources to locate the required resource.
- To launch a resource, simply click once on its row on the screen.

Navigation

The resources (poster pages, photocopiable pages and interactive activities) all open in separate windows on top of the menu screen. This means that you can have more than one resource open at the same time. To close a resource, click on the **x** in the top right-hand corner of the screen. To return to the menu screen you can either close or minimise a resource.

Closing a resource will not close the program. However, if you are in a menu screen, then clicking on the **x** will close the program. To return to a previous menu screen, you need to click on the **Back** button.

Whiteboard tools

The CD-ROM comes with its own set of whiteboard tools for use on any whiteboard. These include:

- Pen tool
- Highlighter tool
- Eraser
- Sticky note

Click on the **Tools** button at the foot of the screen to access these tools.

Printing

Print the resources by clicking on the Print button. The photocopiable pages print as full A4 portrait pages, but please note if you have a landscape photocopiable page or poster you need to set the orientation to landscape in your print preferences. The interactive activities will print what is on the screen. For a full A4 printout you need to set the orientation to landscape in your print preferences.

Framework objectives

Chapter	Page	Section	Literacy skills objectives	Strand 1: Develop and use specific vocabulary in different contexts	Strand 6: Recognise a range of prefixes and suffixes, understanding how they modify meaning	Strand 7: Use syntax, context and word structure to build their store of vocabulary as they read for meaning	Strand 7: Explore how different texts appeal to readers using varied sentence structures and descriptive	Strand 9: Make decisions about form and purpose, identify success criteria and use them to	Strand 9: Select and use a range of technical and descriptive vocabulary
Chapter 1	12	Vocabulary for weather words	To explore synonyms and consider their effect on the reader or listener.	✓					✓
Chapter 1	16	Vocabulary for character description	To explore how vocabulary choices vary according to audience and purpose and according to viewpoint.	✓			✓		✓
Chapter 1	20	Synonyms and antonyms for common words	To explore synonyms and antonyms for common words and learn to choose from alternatives, to add precision and variety to writing.	✓		✓	✓		✓
Chapter 1	24	Vocabulary for story settings	To develop a range of vocabulary for story settings using synonyms, and explore contrasts through antonyms.	✓		✓	✓	✓	✓
Chapter 2	35	Words in a context	To collect and explore words related to particular contexts or topics.	✓		✓			✓
Chapter 2	39	Words and meanings	To use context to work out meanings of unfamiliar words. To use dictionaries to find word meanings, definitions and origins.	✓	✓	✓			✓
Chapter 2	43	Old and new words	To explore how new words come into use in a language and others go out of use or change their meanings.	✓	✓	✓			✓
Chapter 2	47	Different meanings	To explore literal and metaphorical meanings of words and phrases.	✓		✓	✓		✓
Chapter 3	58	Adjectives and adverbs	To extend knowledge of appropriate and powerful adjectives.	✓	✓				✓
Chapter 3	62	Verbs	To extend the range of verbs used for particular contexts.	✓		✓			✓
Chapter 3	66	Formal and informal language	To understand that vocabulary choices vary according to purpose and audience. To acquire a range of vocabulary for formal and informal occasions.	✓			✓	✓	✓
Chapter 3	70	Conjunctions and connectives	To extend the range of conjunctions and time connectives used to link clauses and sentences.			✓	✓	✓	✓

Framework objectives

Page	Section	Literacy skills objectives	Strand 1: Develop and use specific vocabulary in different contexts	Strand 6: Recognise a range of prefixes and suffixes, understanding how they modify meaning	Strand 7: Use syntax, context and word structure to build their store of vocabulary as they read for meaning	Strand 7: Explore how different texts appeal to readers using varied sentence structures and descriptive	Strand 9: Make decisions about form and purpose, identify success criteria and use them to	Strand 9: Select and use a range of technical and descriptive vocabulary
81	Geography	To develop a range of vocabulary associated with different types of weather, climate and other natural phenomena.	✓		✓			✓
85	History	To learn historical vocabulary related to chronology, invasion and settlement, and historical enquiry.	✓		✓			✓
89	Mathematics	To learn mathematical vocabulary related to data handling, 2D shapes and operations.	✓	✓	✓			
93	Science	To learn vocabulary related to investigations in science, materials and healthy eating topics.	✓		✓			
104	Signs and symbols	To learn that signs and symbols sometimes replace words to represent and communicate ideas and meanings. To learn to 'read' a range of common signs and symbols.	✓	✓	✓		✓	✓
108	New words	To learn that portmanteau words are invented by blending parts of two words to make a new word that combines the sense of both.	✓					
112	Collocations and similes	To learn how words are commonly linked together in collocations and similes.	✓			✓		✓
116	Playing with meaning	To learn that the sounds of some words imitate their meanings.	✓			✓		✓

Chapter 4 (pages 81–93)   Chapter 5 (pages 104–116)

Using vocabulary

Using and developing children's vocabulary

Use these notes to support the teaching of vocabulary in this book.

Specific word instruction

Although reading is a valuable means of acquiring new vocabulary, children with weaker vocabularies are less likely to learn new words from reading or from listening to others read. Direct teaching of individual words is therefore most important for children with less word knowledge. Identifying and teaching selected words from a text before reading is one valuable approach to support comprehension. Children need frequent and multiple exposure to a new word to fully comprehend it and assimilate it into their own vocabulary. A word needs to be seen and used in different contexts. Classifying words into different types of 'word family' helps children make connections and predict meanings of unknown words. For example, synonyms and antonyms help children see what a word means and what it does not mean. Children learn the function of a word and how it is used by hearing it and using it in different sentences. Definitions and explanations of new words should be given in everyday language, using words already known and in ways that relate to the children's own experience. Subject-specific and technical vocabulary is crucial for real understanding of concepts, but it needs to be used alongside everyday language until it is fully understood.

Word learning strategies

Children need to learn to use dictionaries effectively to find meanings of unknown words. However, dictionary definitions may use other unknown words and reading a definition does not tell us how a word is used. We still need examples in context. A thesaurus is a valuable source of alternative words, but children need to learn to choose between words with similar meanings by using them in context and evaluating different shades of meaning. Work on word roots and affixes teaches children to analyse words in their parts and make connections in meaning between words with the same parts, such as care, careful and careless. Similarly the etymology (origins) of words helps children see meaning relationships. For example, understanding the origins of the parts enables the meaning of words such as telephone, telescope and television to be predicted. Children also need to learn how to predict a meaning from the context in which a word appears, using their knowledge of how words work in sentences and the subject matter of the text.

Which words to teach?

There are three types of words that children need to learn.

Important words: Firstly, children need to learn words that are important for understanding text, words that will be encountered often and words that relate to specific curriculum areas.

Useful words: Secondly, they need to learn useful words, words that they are likely to be able to put to use in speaking and writing in relevant, age-appropriate contexts.

Difficult words: Thirdly, they need to be taught the difficult words, the ones that they are less likely to work out for themselves, such as idiomatic expressions, words with multiple meanings (such as homonyms), and words that have both everyday and technical meanings (such as *difference* in mathematics).

EAL

Good strategies for children learning EAL are good strategies for all. However, some additional strategies may be needed. Pre-reading vocabulary teaching will be even more important for children learning EAL, as will revisiting previous learning regularly and frequently. If appropriate, a child's home language may be encouraged to make the link between the known and the unknown. Meanings can be reinforced with gestures, pictures and objects. These are not specifically provided or described in this book, but many activities can be supported in this way.

Chapter 1
Synonyms and antonyms

This chapter focuses on the development of vocabulary through an exploration of synonyms and antonyms. The children will investigate shades of meaning of synonyms and learn to select an appropriate word from alternatives. A range of fiction (fables and mystery stories), poetry (performance and language play) and non-fiction reports will help the children develop a sense of audience and voice for writing and for spoken language in different contexts.

Poster notes

Synonyms for good and bad (page 11)
The poster provides a selection of alternatives for *good* and *bad*, grouped according to context, which the children might use in speech or writing. It can be used as a prompt for photocopiable page 22 'A sad poem' and then as a reference for future work. The children can discuss the overlap between categories and the relative strength of individual words.
The poster also offers the opportunity to explore antonyms formed with the affixes 'un-', 'dis-', '-ful' and '-less'. The children can add extra words and categories as they encounter them.

In this chapter

Vocabulary for weather page 12	To explore synonyms and consider their effect on the reader or listener.
Vocabulary for character description page 16	To explore how vocabulary choices vary according to audience and purpose and according to viewpoint.
Synonyms and antonyms for common words page 20	To explore synonyms and antonyms for common words and learn to choose from alternatives, to add precision and variety to writing.
Vocabulary for story settings page 24	To develop a range of vocabulary for story settings using synonyms, and explore contrasts through antonyms.
Assessment page 28	Activities and ideas to assess understanding of the terms *synonym* and *antonym*, and to generate synonyms and antonyms for common words.

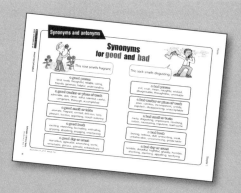

Synonyms and antonyms

Synonyms for good and bad

This sock smells disgusting.

This rose smells fragrant.

a bad person
evil, cruel, mean, naughty, wicked, disagreeable, thoughtless, unreliable

a bad worker or piece of work
poor, careless, incompetent, untidy, slapdash, disappointing, unacceptable

a bad smell or taste
nasty, disgusting, unpleasant, revolting, rotten, nauseating, repulsive, loathsome

a bad book
boring, tedious, dull, unexciting, weak, unbelievable, unconvincing, predictable

a bad day or event
terrible, dreadful, frightful, ghastly, horrible, shocking, alarming, appalling, terrifying

a good person
kind, lovely, thoughtful, reliable, caring, friendly, generous, helpful, understanding

a good worker or piece of work
admirable, able, clever, skilful, talented, careful, competent, thorough, accomplished

a good smell or taste
aromatic, fragrant, scented, delicious, tasty, pleasant, luscious, appetising, mouth-watering

a good book
exciting, interesting, fascinating, enthralling, gripping, absorbing, engaging, entertaining

a good day or event
marvellous, agreeable, astonishing, terrific, remarkable, glorious, splendid, extraordinary

Illustrations © 2010, Woody Fox.

Vocabulary for weather

To explore synonyms and consider their effect on the reader or listener.

Background knowledge

Each of these three texts is about the wind, but each writer has selected vocabulary appropriate to the purpose and audience of the writing. Admiral Sir Francis Beaufort created the Beaufort scale of wind speeds and their effects in 1805 to help sailors estimate the winds through visual observations. In this case, each description had to mean the same to each observer. Although also reporting facts about the wind, the writer of the newspaper article has selected a range of powerful nouns, adjectives and verbs to build atmosphere and engage the reader. The language of the poem imitates the sounds and sensations of wind, using onomatopoeic rhythm and sound patterns, such as *flutter*, *mutter*, *swish* and *creak*.

Activities

These activities explore choices of vocabulary to describe the wind for different purposes and audiences.

● **Photocopiable page 13 'The power of wind'**
Before reading the text, ask the children to describe or act out their interpretations of the wind descriptions. Share background information about the purpose of the Beaufort scale. Encourage the children to extend their vocabulary using their own ideas and a thesaurus to explore shades of meaning of synonyms. Extend the writing activity into drama, using the conditions described as a starting point.

● **Photocopiable page 14 'The Great Storm'**
Read the text to the children first to support comprehension of the challenging vocabulary. Ask them to consider the effect of the words chosen by the writer, such as *shrieked* rather than *blew*. Encourage the children to use a thesaurus to find further powerful words to describe the storm and its effects. Ask them to evaluate the vocabulary choices of others' role plays.

● **Photocopiable page 15 'When the wind blows'**
Encourage the children to read the poem aloud to appreciate the onomatopoeic effect of the verbs that the poet has selected. The children can use some of the words from the poem and add their own to create a rhythmic rap. Extend this by adding sound effects using percussion instruments and everyday objects. Explore antonyms, starting with *haven* and *battle* from the poem.

Further ideas

● **Audience and purpose:** Compare the audience and purpose of the three texts. Who are the intended readers? What are the writers trying to achieve? How does the vocabulary help to achieve this? Let the children rewrite the article using less powerful words and consider the effect.

● **Whatever the weather:** Explore the range of vocabulary that can be used to describe other weather, such as rain or thunderstorms. Ask the children to create posters with pictures and word banks.

● **Opposites:** Find synonyms for *hot* and order them according to hotness (which may be subjective). Repeat for *cold* and explore antonyms.

What's on the CD-ROM

On the CD-ROM you will find:
● Printable versions of all three photocopiable pages.
● Answers to 'The power of wind' and 'The Great Storm'.
● Interactive versions of 'The Great Storm' and 'When the wind blows'.

Vocabulary for weather

The power of wind

■ Below is the Beaufort scale, which describes different strengths of wind. Underline the 'wind words' (such as **breeze** and **gentle**) and make a list in your book or on the back of this sheet.

■ Use a thesaurus to find other words and phrases to describe the wind.

■ Group together words that have the same or similar meanings. Put them in order of strength.

■ Use your sets of words to write a description of a storm as it grows more powerful.

Beaufort number	Description	Land conditions
0	Calm	Calm. Smoke rises vertically.
1	Light air	Smoke moves a little.
2	Light breeze	Leaves rustle. Wind felt on exposed skin.
3	Gentle breeze	Leaves and smaller twigs in constant motion.
4	Moderate breeze	Small branches begin to move. Dust and loose paper raised.
5	Fresh breeze	Branches of a moderate size move. Smaller trees sway.
6	Strong breeze	Large branches move. Becomes difficult to use an umbrella.
7	Near gale	Whole trees move. Effort needed to walk against the wind.
8	Gale	Twigs broken from trees. Cars veer on road.
9	Severe gale	Larger branches break off trees and some small trees blow over. Damage to canvas structures.
10	Storm	Trees uprooted. Tiles come off roofs.
11	Violent storm	Widespread structural damage to roofs and temporary buildings.
12	Hurricane	Massive and widespread damage to windows and weaker buildings. Debris may be hurled about.

Name:

Vocabulary for weather

The Great Storm

■ Read this newspaper article about a storm that struck southern England in October 1987.

■ Highlight the words that show how powerful the storm was and how much damage was caused.

■ Underneath the article, write words that describe how you would feel in a storm like this.

■ Work with a partner to prepare an interview between a reporter and a witness who experienced the storm.

The Great Storm

Winds exceeding 100 miles per hour caused the worst damage ever known to any living person in southern England during the small hours of 16th October.

In a few hours, the Great Storm carved a swathe across southern England, leaving a trail of death and destruction. Many people who had cowered in their beds as the storm passed over their homes woke to scenes of unthinkable devastation.

With gusts reaching 115 miles per hour the storm shrieked across the country and in its wake left 18 people dead, 15 million trees uprooted and an insurance bill running into billions.

One ferocious night wrecked fences, power lines, cars, mobile homes and houses and reduced Shanklin Pier on the Isle of Wight to a pile of flotsam. In Kent, which bore much of the storm's anger, Sevenoaks lost six of the trees that gave the town its name.

Storms of this magnitude can normally be predicted in advance. However, the unexpected movements of this storm caught even the meteorologists by surprise, showing that you can never trust the weather.

When the wind blows

■ Underneath the poem write down the words the poet uses to talk about the sights and sounds of a windy day. Read them aloud and notice the onomatopoeia.

■ Which other words could you use to describe this type of weather? Use a thesaurus if you need to.

■ Put some of your words into pairs like the poet has done. Think about the sounds and meanings of the words.

■ Practise reading aloud your pairs of words as an onomatopoeia rap.

When the wind blows

When the wind blows
Coats flap, scarves flutter.
When the wind blows
Branches groan, leaves mutter.
When the wind blows
Curtains swish, papers scatter.
When the wind blows
Gates creak, dustbins clatter.
When the wind blows
Doors slam, windows rattle.
When the wind blows
Inside is a haven,
Outside is a battle.

John Foster

_____

_____

_____

_____

_____

_____

_____

SCHOLASTIC
www.scholastic.co.uk   **PHOTOCOPIABLE**   Scholastic Literacy Skills
Vocabulary: Year 3   15

Vocabulary for character description

To explore how vocabulary choices vary according to audience and purpose and according to viewpoint.

Background knowledge

A fable is a short story with a clear moral message that aims to teach the reader a lesson about life. The characters are often animals that display distinct, usually contrasting, human characteristics, such as *wise/foolish* or *lazy/industrious*. Settings are rarely described because characters are more important. However, because fables are short, there is little character development and the reader has to read between the lines to understand characters and motives. Looking at a story from different points of view enables the children to adapt their vocabulary choices for different voices.

Activities

The children will develop their vocabulary to describe characters through a narrative, a dialogue and a poem based on the fable 'The Cricket and the Ant'.

● **Photocopiable page 17 'The Ant and the Cricket (1)'**

At first, the children will consider the obvious character traits prompted by the words suggested. The behaviour of the ant at the end, however, may generate other vocabulary, such as *mean* or *unkind*. Encourage the children to note that words can have a lot of synonyms, but that no two have exactly the same meaning. The same word may also have different antonyms.

● **Photocopiable page 18 'The Ant and the Cricket (2)'**

Challenge the children to use vocabulary from the first activity to bring the characters to life in dialogue. They should work in pairs to write and perform their dialogues. The activity could be purely oral, with the children improvising dialogue, although encourage them to tell the story rather than simply exchange insults.

● **Photocopiable page 19 'The Ant and the Cricket (3)'**

Before asking the children to prepare performances, explore the voices of the poem by reading it aloud. Note a slightly different viewpoint, created by vocabulary such as *miserly ant* and *poor little cricket*.

Further ideas

● **Point of view:** Tell other well-known stories from different points of view and explore how the vocabulary changes according to the voice.

● **Animal characteristics:** Invite the children to make character posters for this and other fables, collecting a bank of descriptive vocabulary for character development. Let the children write their own animal fables, selecting two animals with opposite characteristics.

● **Stereotypes:** Explore the stereotypes commonly found in fables and other stories, such as the wise owl or cunning fox, developing a bank of common adjective or noun pairings. Some of the children may enjoy subverting these stereotypes in stories.

 **What's on the CD-ROM**

On the CD-ROM you will find:
● Printable versions of all three photocopiable pages.
● Interactive version of 'The Ant and the Cricket (1)'.

Vocabulary for character description

The Ant and the Cricket (1)

In a field one summer's day a cricket was hopping about, singing cheerfully. An ant passed by, carrying an ear of corn he was taking to the nest. The cricket laughed at the ant and asked why he didn't just enjoy the sunshine while he could. The ant replied that he had to store up food for the winter, when the ground would be frozen and there would be nothing to eat. The cricket just carried on dancing, saying that there was lots of time to worry about the winter. So all through the summer, the ant worked while the cricket played. One morning the cricket woke up shivering. He looked outside and saw that the ground was covered with snow. He searched everywhere for something to eat but he could find nothing. At last the cricket knocked on the ant's door and asked him to share some of his food. The ant asked why he didn't gather food in the summer and the cricket replied that he was too busy dancing and singing. So the ant sent him away to dance and sing the winter away.

The moral of the story: *A wise person always plans ahead.*

■ Look at the words below. Which do you think describe the cricket and which describe the ant? Write the words under the correct heading in the chart below. Think about which words have similar meanings and which have opposite meanings.

	careful	silly	lazy	sensible
clever	irresponsible	hard-working	idle	busy

■ On another piece of paper, draw a picture of the cricket and a picture of the ant.

■ Write other words to describe the two creatures around your pictures of the cricket and ant. Use your own ideas and a thesaurus.

Words that describe the cricket	Words that describe the ant

Illustrations © 2010, Woody Fox.

   PHOTOCOPIABLE   Scholastic Literacy Skills
Vocabulary: Year 3   **17**

Name:

The Ant and the Cricket (2)

■   This is the beginning of the fable of the cricket and the ant. It is a dialogue between the two main characters. It is written like a play.

Hey Ant, you look hot and bothered. What are you up to?

I'm collecting food for the winter.

Cricket: Hey Ant, you look hot and bothered. What are you up to?
Ant: I'm collecting food for the winter.
Cricket: Are you mad? It's too hot to work. Come and play.

■   Write the rest of the story as a playscript. Think about what you know about the two characters. Use some of the words you found to describe them. Sometimes you might want to write what Cricket or Ant is thinking.

Ant: _____

_____

_____

_____

_____

_____

_____

_____

_____

_____

_____

_____

Illustrations © 2010, Woody Fox.

Vocabulary for character description

The Ant and the Cricket (3)

■ Work in groups of three (narrator, cricket and ant) to prepare a performance of the poem. Use the clues in the poem and what you know about the characters to bring the poem to life.

A silly young cricket, accustomed to sing
Through the warm, sunny months of gay summer and spring,
Began to complain, when he found that at home
His cupboard was empty and winter was come.
Not a crumb to be found
On the snow-covered ground;
Not a flower could he see,
Not a leaf on a tree.
"Oh, what will become," says the cricket, "of me?"
At last by starvation and famine made bold,
All dripping with wet and all trembling with cold,
Away he set off to a miserly ant
To see if, to keep him alive, he would grant
Him shelter from rain.
A mouthful of grain
He wished only to borrow,
He'd repay it tomorrow;
If not helped, he must die of starvation and sorrow.
Says the ant to the cricket: "I'm your servant and friend,
But we ants never borrow, we ants never lend.
Pray tell me, dear sir, did you lay nothing by
When the weather was warm?" Said the cricket, "Not I.
My heart was so light
That I sang day and night,
For all nature looked gay."
"You sang, sir, you say?
Go then," said the ant, "and sing winter away."
Thus ending, he hastily lifted the wicket
And out of the door turned the poor little cricket.
Though this is a fable, the moral is good –
If you live without work, you must live without food.

Anonymous

SCHOLASTIC
www.scholastic.co.uk   **PHOTOCOPIABLE**   **Scholastic Literacy Skills**
Vocabulary: Year 3   **19**

Synonyms and antonyms for common words

Objective

To explore synonyms and antonyms for common words and learn to choose from alternatives, to add precision and variety to writing.

Background knowledge

The children should be encouraged to use a variety of words in their writing, not just to avoid repetition and add interest, but to convey more precisely their intended meaning to the reader and develop their sense of audience. Many words used by young or inexperienced writers, such as *good*, *nice*, *said* and *went*, are imprecise and can convey many different meanings. Synonyms do not carry identical meanings and alternatives need to be selected carefully according to the context. Antonyms are commonly defined as opposites and while some are exactly that, many pairs, such as *happy* and *sad*, also have degrees or types of happiness or sadness.

Activities

Synonyms for *good* and *sad* are explored in the context of a book review and a poem. Synonyms for other common words, including *nice*, *went* and *said*, are considered in a short story.

● **Photocopiable page 21 'Book review'**
Before reading the text, raise awareness of the many different meanings for *good* by generating synonyms in a range of phrases, such as *a good film*, *a good smell* and *a good writer*. Note that *a good boy* has a distinctly different meaning. Model how to select appropriate synonyms in thesauruses. Encourage the children to read their reviews to check that they have chosen appropriate words. Let the children use the text as a model for their own book reviews.

● **Photocopiable page 22 'A sad poem'**
Discuss the shades of meaning in each of the synonyms for *sad*. Ask the children to share with a partner something that makes them sad, gloomy, miserable, and so on. Use shared writing to begin a *happy* poem using the same model.

● **Photocopiable page 23 'The day I met a giant'**
Here the children will explore the effect of verbs and adjectives in a story. To use a thesaurus effectively, the children will need to be aware of past tenses: *saw* (*see*), *went* (*go*), *came* (*come*), *said* (*say*). Ask the children to evaluate each other's rewritten short stories.

Further ideas

● **Word bank:** From personal and shared reading, collect alternatives for *good*. Let the children develop their own word banks or contribute to a class bank, perhaps grouping into words with similar meanings. Explore synonyms for other common words, such as *bad*, *great*, *nice*, *big* and *small*.

● **Opposites poems:** Choose other antonym pairs, such as *quiet/loud*, *light/dark*, to write synonym poems using a similar model.

● **Better words:** Use drama to explore alternatives for other common verbs, such as *run*, *eat* and *look*. Let the children work in groups, each member miming a synonym for the chosen word.

 **What's on the CD-ROM**

On the CD-ROM you will find:
● Printable versions of all three photocopiable pages.
● Interactive versions of 'A sad poem' and 'The day I met a giant'.

Book review

■ Choose one of the words in the box (or one of your own) to replace the bold word **good** in this book review. Rewrite the review, using your new words, in your book or on a piece of paper.

wonderful	delightful	fascinating	valuable
extraordinary	useful	amusing	tasty
clever	excellent	exciting	entertaining
enjoyable		interesting	

Book review by Harry Shore

Book title: *The Owl who was Afraid of the Dark*
Author: Jill Tomlinson

What happens in the book?
Plop is a baby barn owl and he has lots of **good** adventures. He meets some **good** characters and learns some **good** things about the dark.

Which were your favourite things about the book?
It is **good** when Plop falls off his branch and when his dad brings him something **good** for supper. The chapter where the man with the telescope shows Plop different stars is **good**. There are some **good** words in the book. There are lots of **good** pictures too.

Would you recommend the book to other people?
It was a really **good** book and I'm sure other people will think it's **good** too. It's a **good** book for the children who are afraid of the dark. I think Jill Tomlinson is a very **good** writer. I am going to read some of her other books and I hope they are as **good** as this one.

Illustrations © 2010, Woody Fox.

Name:

A sad poem

■ Read the poem and underline the synonyms for **sad**.
■ Write them in the box below and add **three** more words.

Sad is losing your favourite toy.
Gloomy is being indoors on a damp winter day.
Miserable is when she's not your best friend any more.
Fed up is having no one to play with.
Upset is not being picked for the team.
Tearful is your first day in a new school.

■ **Happy** is an antonym of **sad**. Think of words that mean **happy** and write them in the box. Use a thesaurus to help.

Sad words	Happy words
sad	
gloomy	

■ Write your own poem about happy feelings. Think about things that make you happy. Choose the best happy word for each idea.

_____

_____

_____

_____

_____

_____

_____

Illustrations © 2010, Woody Fox.

PHOTOCOPIABLE ■SCHOLASTIC
www.scholastic.co.uk

Synonyms and antonyms for common words

The day I met a giant

It was a **nice** day. I was feeling **happy**.
I went for a **walk** in the woods.
Then I met a giant. He was **big**. I was **scared**.
I **went** up a tree. The giant **came** closer.
He **saw** me. "Found you," he **said**.
"Now it's my turn to hide and you can seek!"

■ Can you make this story more exciting? Find at least three synonyms for each of the highlighted words. Choose the best one to improve the story. Write your new story in your book or on a piece of paper.

nice _____

happy _____

walk _____

big _____

scared _____

went _____

came _____

saw _____

said _____

Illustrations © 2010, Woody Fox.

Vocabulary for story settings

Objective

To develop a range of vocabulary for story settings using synonyms, and explore contrasts through antonyms.

Background knowledge

The focus in this section is the vocabulary of story settings, but the ideas could be used for other contexts, such as character development. Settings establish where and when a story takes place and are important in creating mood and atmosphere. Settings can be familiar places, such as school or a shopping centre, or unfamiliar with an inbuilt air of strangeness or menace, such as a derelict or uninhabited house. The activities explore a range of settings, developing a vocabulary of sights, sounds, smells and feelings, which is crucial in establishing the desired effects and impressions.

Activities

The first two activities are based on contrasting locations, developing knowledge of both synonyms and antonyms, while the third focuses on a setting that might appear in a mystery story.

● **Photocopiable page 25 'Story settings'**
Ask the children to close their eyes as you read each text extract, to imagine the setting and discuss any words that give them clues about it. Can the children draw the settings from the descriptions before they start the activity? Extend the vocabulary by encouraging the children to find synonyms for the suggested words.

● **Photocopiable page 26 'Contrasting settings'**
Ask the children to use their own ideas first and then provide thesauruses to develop the vocabulary. Use

the plenary to group words with similar meanings and to discuss antonyms (*dark/dismal* and *bright/colourful*; *welcoming* and *forbidding*).

● **Photocopiable page 27 'Word webs'**
The children may have used concept maps for other topics. This activity encourages them to think as broadly as possible in the initial stages of planning and describing a setting. They can then select the most appropriate or powerful words to write descriptions.

Further ideas

● **Powerful description:** Invite the children to finish the sentences *I could see…* and *I could hear…* Encourage more confident learners to vary their sentences to add interest and impact, such as *Green mould grew up the slimy walls*.

● **Settings word banks:** Collect further vocabulary from shared and personal reading for a range of different settings. Use pictures of other locations, both familiar and mysterious, such as school, the supermarket, caves and desert islands, to generate a class collection of vocabulary for story settings. The children could describe the same setting at different times of day or in different seasons.

● **Character description:** Use similar activities to develop the children's vocabulary for describing characters in stories. Use villains and heroes from popular fiction to explore synonyms and antonyms.

● **Mystery stories:** Develop the work into writing more extended mystery stories. Encourage the children to explore the possibilities for mystery in both familiar and unfamiliar settings.

 What's on the CD-ROM

On the CD-ROM you will find:
● Printable versions of all three photocopiable pages.

Vocabulary for story settings

Story settings

- ■ Read these story settings.
- ■ Choose words from the box below that you think best describe each setting. You can use words as many times as you like. Then add other words of your own.
- ■ Underline the words in the texts that helped you decide.

The barn was very large. It was old. It smelled of hay and it smelled of manure. It smelled of the perspiration of tired horses and the wonderful sweet breath of patient cows. It had a sort of peaceful smell – as if nothing bad could happen ever again in the world.

From *Charlotte's Web* by EB White

_____

_____

I nearly got into the garage that Sunday morning… Everything was covered in dust and spiders' webs. There was mortar that had fallen from the walls. There was a little window in one of the walls but it was filthy and there were rolls of cracked lino standing in front of it. The place stank of rot and dust.

From *Skellig* by David Almond

_____

_____

There were other trees in the garden, and one of the things which made the place look strangest and loveliest was that climbing roses had run all over them and swung down long tendrils which made light swaying curtains…

From *The Secret Garden*
by Frances Hodgson Burnett

_____

_____

strange   cheerful   dismal   lovely   scary
ordinary   peaceful   gloomy   deserted
friendly   safe   mysterious   menacing
exciting   cosy

Skellig text © 1998, David Almond; Charlotte's Web text © 1952, EB White; illustrations © 2010, Woody Fox.

Name:

Contrasting settings

■ Around each house, write all the words you can think of to describe it. Then use a thesaurus to find more.

lonely

spooky

dark

forbidding

colourful

welcoming

cheerful

bright

Illustrations © 2010, Woody Fox.

Word webs

■ When you want to describe a setting try to use as many words as you can. Think about what you might see, hear, smell, touch and feel.

■ Add more ideas to this deserted house word web. Don't stop until the paper is full!

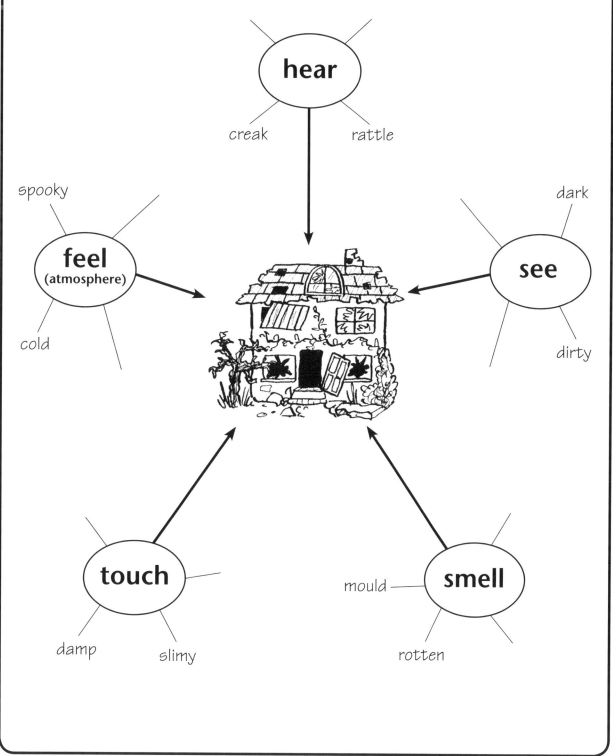

Illustrations © 2010, Woody Fox.

Assessment

The following grid shows the main objectives and activities covered in this chapter. You can use the grid to locate activities that cover a particular focus that you are keen to monitor.

Objective	Page	Activity title
To explore synonyms and consider their effect on the reader or listener.	13 14 15	The power of wind The Great Storm When the wind blows
To explore how vocabulary choices vary according to audience and purpose and according to viewpoint.	17 18 19	The Ant and the Cricket (1) The Ant and the Cricket (2) The Ant and the Cricket (3)
To explore synonyms and antonyms for common words and learn to choose from alternatives, to add precision and variety to writing.	21 22 23	Book review A sad poem The day I met a giant
To develop a range of vocabulary for story settings using synonyms, and explore contrasts through antonyms.	25 26 27	Story settings Contrasting settings Word webs

Observation and record keeping

Assessment should track the children's development in both knowledge and skills. Record the children's areas of strength and targets for development in the following areas:
- ability to use the terms *synonym* and *antonym*
- ability to generate synonyms and antonyms

- range of vocabulary used (in speech and in writing) in a given context
- ability to select an appropriate word from possible alternatives in a particular context
- awareness of the effect of vocabulary choices on audience
- understanding of the purpose and organisation of a thesaurus
- ability to use a thesaurus to find synonyms.

Assessment activity

- **What you need**
Photocopiable page 29 'Synonyms and antonyms', appropriate thesauruses.
- **What to do**
The activity assesses the children's understanding of the terms *synonym* and *antonym*, their ability to generate them and to use them appropriately. The children should be able to work independently. If wanted, allow the children to try words on small whiteboards before recording on the sheet. Either let the children work without a thesaurus to assess their knowledge of word alternatives, or with a thesaurus to assess their effective use of it.

Differentiation

- Explain the words *synonym* and *antonym* if necessary. Less confident learners might work orally, with an adult scribing their responses. Provide a word bank of relevant words.
- Challenge more confident learners to use more of their synonyms and/or antonyms in sentences to assess their ability to distinguish between meanings in different contexts and shades of meaning.

Further learning

- **Adventurous vocabulary:** Encourage the children to be adventurous with vocabulary choices in writing, but to be aware of the audience when selecting from alternatives.
- **Thesaurus:** Develop effective use of a thesaurus, encouraging the children to be aware of subtle differences in meaning between synonyms.
- **Display:** Celebrate particularly exciting and appropriate words in a display.

Assessment

Synonyms and antonyms

■ Write three synonyms and three antonyms for each of these words.

	Synonyms	Antonyms
sad		
big		
dark		
good		

■ Choose one of your synonyms for each word and write each one in a sentence.

(sad) _____

_____

_____

(big) _____

_____

_____

(dark) _____

_____

_____

(good) _____

_____

_____

Word of the week

The Word of the week pages provide information on one word linked to each section in the chapter. Each word is described in some of the following categories: word definition, word origin, word family, alternative words, fascinating facts and activities. Not all categories are relevant to every word.

You can use the words as a focus to support your work on the different sections of the chapter. For example, you could create a display around it. The information is a starting point for a word focus. The words could form part of your classroom living word bank.

You could also use the word of the week as a springboard to inspire children to think about or research fascinating facts about words, find interesting quotations and to encourage them to use dictionaries and thesauruses.

Wind

● **Word definition:** A noun meaning moving air.
● **Word origin:** From the Latin *ventus*, meaning wind.
● **Word family:** Verb: *wind* (*to wind a baby*), *winding*, *winded*; adjective: *windy*; adverb: *windily*; noun: *windiness*.
● **Alternative words:** Breeze, cyclone, draught, gale, gust, hurricane, squall.
● **Fascinating facts:** Wind is a renewable energy source. Modern-day turbines take the wind and turn it into electricity. Wind also used to be used by windmills to ground grain to make flour.
● **Activities:** Ask the children to investigate the meanings of compound words and phrases, such as *wind instrument*, *windmill*, *windbreak*, *windpipe*, *windsock*, *wind tunnel*, *windswept*, *windfall*, *wind farm* and *wind chime*; metaphorical expressions, such as *put the wind up*, *get wind of*, *in the wind*, *take the wind out of someone's sails*, *sail close to the wind*, *second wind* and *wind of change*.

> Linked section: Vocabulary for weather, page 12

Fabulous

● **Word definition:** An adjective meaning excellent.
● **Word origin:** From *fable*, from the Latin *fabula*, meaning story.
● **Word family:** Noun: *fable*; adjective: *fabled*; adverb: *fabulously*.
● **Alternative words:** Brilliant, fantastic, magnificent, marvellous, splendid, superb, terrific, wonderful.
● **Fascinating facts:** The meaning of *fabulous* has moved from its original sense of 'spoken or written about in a fable', that is 'imaginary or impossible to believe', to its colloquial meaning today of really good.
● **Activities:** It is a valuable synonym in writing, but should be used with an awareness of its original sense, as in *a fabulous castle* or *a giant with fabulous strength*. Investigate other words that have changed their meanings, such as *terrific* (literally terrifying), *stupendous* (stunned), *brilliant* (shining) and *awesome* (full of awe) and try to use them in these senses in writing. Investigate the similarly extended uses of other derivations: *fabled* (from the same root), *mythical* and *legendary*.

> Linked section: Vocabulary for character description, page 16

Extraordinary

- **Word definition:** An adjective meaning remarkable or wonderful.
- **Word origin:** From the Latin *extra* (outside) and *ordinary* (from *ordo*, meaning order), in total meaning outside the usual order or custom.
- **Word family:** Adverb: extraordinarily; noun: extraordinariness.
- **Alternative words:** Amazing, exceptional, outstanding, sensational, mysterious, peculiar, strange, surprising, unusual.
- **Fascinating facts:** Modern uses of *extra* can suggest a meaning of 'especially', as in *extra-special*, which could lead to an opposite meaning for *extraordinary* as 'especially ordinary'.

> **Linked section:** Synonyms and antonyms for common words, page 20

- **Activities:** Explore other words using the prefix *extra* to understand its meaning of 'outside': *extraterrestrial*, *extracurricular*, *extrasensory*. It is a word that the children seem to enjoy the sound of. Encourage them to use it as often as possible in as many contexts as possible, such as *Extraordinary weather today*, *What an extraordinary piece of writing*, *An extraordinary story*, *An extraordinarily interesting history lesson*. Award points every time a child manages to get it into a discussion or piece of writing.

Atmosphere

- **Word definition:** A noun meaning the feel of a place or the surrounding influence or environment.
- **Word origin:** From the Greek *atmos* (vapour) and *sphaira* (sphere), meaning the gaseous envelope that surrounds the earth or any of the celestial bodies.
- **Word family:** Adjective: *atmospheric*.
- **Alternative words:** Ambience, aura, feeling, mood.
- **Fascinating facts:** The literal meaning of the word is scientific, but it is used metaphorically as in *an atmosphere of hostility*.

> **Linked section:** Vocabulary for story settings, page 24

- **Activities:** Use the word *atmosphere* in different contexts: the atmosphere in the classroom, assembly or playground at different times of the day; the atmosphere of a painting or piece of music. Encourage the children to think about how the setting makes them feel, using a range of vocabulary and explaining what creates a particular atmosphere.

Fun with words

Use these activities to support the vocabulary work in this chapter. They could be used as starter or plenary activities.

Synonym game
● Divide the children into mixed-ability groups. Give them a common word, such as *big*, and ask them to find as many synonyms as possible in a given time. Give one point for each valid synonym. Either give a thesaurus to each group or ask the children to come up with their own ideas. Vary the activity by only awarding points for a synonym that no other group has suggested. You could also play the 'Synonym game' with antonyms.

Pairs
● Make sets of paired cards, using either synonyms or antonyms. Ask the children to work in pairs or small groups to sort the cards into pairs of synonyms or antonyms. Turn the cards face down and let the children take turns to turn over two cards, keeping them if they are a pair. Hand out the cards and ask the children to find and sit with their matching pair. Encourage them to try to find more words that fit their starting pair.

Shades of meaning
● Tell the children to work in groups of three and give each group a set of three synonyms. Ask them to order the synonyms according to shades of meaning and then prepare a role play to illustrate the range of meanings.

Headwords
● Prepare sets of cards, each with a headword (a common word such as *sad* and *great*) and three synonyms. Call out the headword and ask each group to suggest a synonym. Award points if a group has selected a synonym that is not on the card. Try the same activity for antonyms.

Unmentionable
● Prepare cards that contain a headword and several other words connected to it. The children take turns to pick a card and describe the headword for a partner to guess without using any of the other words on the card. For example, the headword might be *ruler* and the unmentionable words *long*, *measure*, *straight* and *line*. This encourages the children to find alternative vocabulary.

Forbidden words
● Prepare 'context' cards and 'forbidden words'. For example, contexts might include: *Tell me about your best friend*, *what you did at the weekend*, *your favourite footballer*, *your favourite film*, *the book you are reading at the moment*. Forbidden words might be *great*, *nice*, *good* and *brilliant*. The children work with a partner, taking turns to choose a context for their partner to talk about without using the forbidden words.

Rename the story
● Give pairs or groups of the children a book or story title and ask them to use a thesaurus to rename the story. For example, *Sleeping Beauty* might become *Snoozing Loveliness*. Let the children swap their new titles for others to guess.

Chapter 2

Word families, roots and meanings

Introduction

This chapter encourages the children to see words in family groups and look for connections in form and meaning. A range of relevant contexts and text types will develop the children's curiosity about words, their meanings, their origins and their uses. The children will begin to be aware of the way in which words come and go in language and how meanings change. They can use dictionaries to explore definitions and origins, but will also explore creative ways in which words can be used to express meanings beyond the literal.

Poster notes

Homonyms (page 34)
The poster provides examples of the many homonyms in English. It can be used as an introduction to photocopiable page 41 'Two meanings in one'. It will provide starting points for the children's own ideas on homonyms and for exploring jokes and double meanings (for example, *What type of flower do you find in your eye? An iris*).

In this chapter

Words in a context page 35	To collect and explore words related to particular contexts or topics.
Words and meanings page 39	To use context to work out meanings of unfamiliar words. To use dictionaries to find word meanings, definitions and origins.
Old and new words page 43	To explore how new words come into use in a language and others go out of use or change their meanings.
Different meanings page 47	To explore literal and metaphorical meanings of words and phrases.
Assessment page 51	Activities and ideas to assess the ability to make links in meaning between words with the same affix, and to distinguish between homonyms in context.

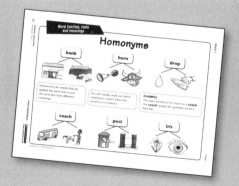

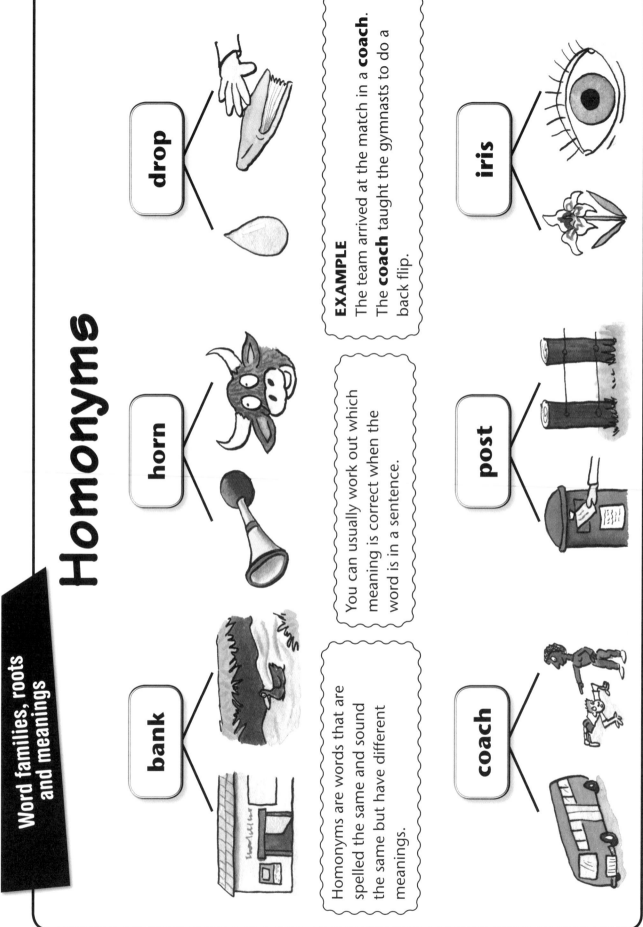

Homonyms

Word families, roots and meanings

drop

horn

bank

EXAMPLE
The team arrived at the match in a **coach**.
The **coach** taught the gymnasts to do a back flip.

You can usually work out which meaning is correct when the word is in a sentence.

Homonyms are words that are spelled the same and sound the same but have different meanings.

iris

post

coach

Illustrations © 2010, Woody Fox.

PHOTOCOPIABLE   ■SCHOLASTIC
www.scholastic.co.uk

Words in a context

Objective

To collect and explore words related to particular contexts or topics.

Background knowledge

The vocabulary related to a particular topic or context is sometimes referred to as a 'field'. The starting point is known as the 'anchor word', which is the word whose links are being explored and to which all other words are related in meaning in some way. Words can be generated by word association, so the anchor prevents you from wandering too far from the central idea. The principle can be extended to a concept map, where words generated from the anchor become the anchor themselves. For example, in the field of *library*, the word *book* can be extended to *cover*, *page*, *chapter*, *title*, *author* and so on. Meaning-based word families are important for vocabulary growth and for consolidation of familiar words.

Activities

Using contexts of the school library, jobs and hobbies or interests, the children will learn that situations and activities have their own fields of specialist language.

● **Photocopiable page 36 'Our school library'**
Begin this activity in the school library to enable the children to generate word lists. Let the children work on larger sheets of paper to fully develop concept maps. Encourage the children to use the vocabulary generated to make labels and posters for the library or class book collections.

● **Photocopiable page 37 'Tools of the trade'**
Although some of the words are tricky, the children will be familiar with many from home, play and television programmes. Let them extend the vocabulary to clothes

where applicable, and find pictures of items for a 'jobs' display. Develop further vocabulary by making sentences, such as *I use a saw to cut wood* or *I listen to a person's heartbeat with a stethoscope*, and then into dialogue and role play.

● **Photocopiable page 38 'What do I do?'**
Where possible, use experts in the class to develop the information in each description. Let the children choose activities or hobbies for the task, such as computer games or music, or a topic of interest, such as dinosaurs.

Further ideas

● **Our school library:** Let the children use their concept maps to write a description of the library for the school brochure or website. If your school library is less than ideal, ask them to describe the library as they would like it to look and operate.
● **Around school:** Ask the children to create concept maps for other areas in school, such as the hall or an art area.
● **Job search:** Research vocabulary related to other jobs, such as teaching. Ask the children to find out and make lists of vocabulary related to adults' jobs. They could describe a job for the rest of the class to name.
● **Personal interests:** Encourage the children to compile glossaries of words related to their own hobbies or interests.

What's on the CD-ROM

On the CD-ROM you will find:
● Printable versions of all three photocopiable pages.
● Answers to 'Tools of the trade' and 'What do I do?'.
● Interactive version of 'Tools of the trade'.

Name:

Our school library

■ These are some words that you might think of when you are talking about the school library. Add more words and ideas to this concept map for **library**.

Shelf

Library

Borrow

Read

Books

fiction
story
adventure

poetry
poet
rhyme

non-fiction
information
facts

PHOTOCOPIABLE ■SCHOLASTIC
www.scholastic.co.uk

Words in a context

Tools of the trade

■ People often need special tools or equipment to do a particular job. Decide which equipment is used by each of these people and write them in the correct boxes. Use a dictionary if you need to.

■ Can you add any more words to the boxes?

nurse	gardener
stethoscope 	
chef 	**carpenter** 

whisk	chisel	spade	~~stethoscope~~	syringe	hoe
hammer		grater	drill	spatula	rake
thermometer	trowel	bandage		colander	screwdriver
peeler	saw	forceps	secateurs		

Illustrations © 2010, Woody Fox.

Name:

Words in a context

What do I do?

■ Here are six children talking about activities they enjoy. Write what the activity is below each speech bubble. Underline the words that helped you decide.

■ Choose an activity that you enjoy. Write down all the words that you use to describe it. Prepare a two-minute talk to tell the rest of the class about it.

I play in a team. Some players are attackers and some are defenders. I usually play in midfield, but last week I was the goalkeeper. I have to pass the ball accurately and mark the player on the other team. I've scored six goals this season.

_____

I play a game on a court with a net across the middle. I play with a racket and can hit the ball on the backhand or the forehand. I am learning to serve and volley. I can play singles with two players or doubles with four players.

_____

I am learning to do different strokes. You have to learn how to breathe properly. I can do front crawl and butterfly. I can dive as well. My little sister is learning to float and she still wears armbands.

_____

I wear a leotard. I can do forward and backward rolls and handstands. Sometimes we do activities on the mat and sometimes on the apparatus. It's very hard to balance on the beam. I like the climbing ropes and the vaulting box.

_____

I have a board with wheels underneath and I wear a helmet and pads on my knees and elbows. I go to a special park with ramps. I can do lots of tricks, like a wheelie and a pivot. An 'ollie' is where you jump and your board goes in the air.

_____

I like doing this because I like music. You have to learn different steps and listen carefully to the rhythm. I used to do jazz and tap but I've just started hip hop.

_____

Illustrations © 2010, Woody Fox.

■SCHOLASTIC
www.scholastic.co.uk

Words and meanings

Objectives

To use context to work out meanings of unfamiliar words. To use dictionaries to find word meanings, definitions and origins.

Background knowledge

When children come across a word they do not recognise on sight, they first have to decode it to know what it says. They may then need to work out its meaning using the clues in the text, including the grammar and context. If the meaning cannot be deciphered, encourage the children to use dictionaries. Homonyms are words with the same spelling and pronunciation, but two meanings. The correct meaning can usually be determined from the context. Knowledge of the origins of words and of affixes and their meanings can help the children work out meanings from root words.

Activities

The children work out meanings of unfamiliar words in a Greek myth, explore double meanings in a poem based on homonyms and work out meanings of words with the same prefixes.

● **Photocopiable page 40 'Meanings in context'**
Let the children work in pairs to work out meanings and think of alternative words before using dictionaries. Use the plenary to evaluate the children's new versions. Discuss the impact of simplified vocabulary on the overall effect of the passage.

● **Photocopiable page 41 'Two meanings in one'**
Discuss examples of homonyms using poster page 34 'Homonyms'. Note that the two meanings can be found in a dictionary, but you can only tell which one is

meant once the words are in sentences. Read the poem aloud and discuss the first two or three images. Invite the children to draw pictures. Ask them to find other homonyms and write questions as in the poem.

● **Photocopiable page 42 'Dictionary definitions'**
This will encourage the children to look for parts in words (roots and affixes) and recognise similarities in meaning between words with the same parts. Let some of the children use dictionaries to find the etymology of other word parts, such as '-lateral', '-nox' and '-valent'. Encourage the children to try to explain meanings in their own words if they can.

Further ideas

● **Definitions:** Ask the children to write their own definitions of concrete nouns, such as *table*, *pencil* and *dog*. Can the other children work out the words defined? Challenge more confident learners to define verbs (*jump*), abstract nouns (*happiness*) or adjectives (*big*).

● **More prefixes:** Give the children sets of words with the same prefix and ask them to work out what the prefix and the words mean.

● **Using context:** Take opportunities in shared and guided reading to model how to work out word meanings using grammar and context. Ask the children to find homonyms and put them in sentences to show meanings.

What's on the CD-ROM

On the CD-ROM you will find:
● Printable versions of all three photocopiable pages.
● Answers to all three photocopiable pages.
● Interactive version of 'Two meanings in one'.

Name:

Words and meanings

Meanings in context

■ Read this extract from the Greek myth 'Theseus and the Minotaur'.

■ Underline any words you do not know or fully understand. Try to work out what the words mean using the clues in the sentence or other parts of the story.

■ Use a dictionary and a thesaurus to check meanings and find alternative words.

■ On the other side of this sheet or in your book, rewrite the extract, using your alternative words.

Theseus vowed he would kill the Minotaur and he set forth for Crete. King Aegeus deeply cherished Theseus and told him to ensure that the ship he returned in hoisted a white flag indicating his triumph over the Minotaur, rather than the traditional black pennant. When Theseus disembarked from his ship in Crete, he informed King Minos that if he slaughtered the beast, Athens would no longer owe tribute to Crete. If his plan foundered, he would be slain by the Minotaur in the labyrinth. King Minos scoffed at this challenge and, desiring to see Theseus die, allowed him to cross the threshold of the labyrinth.

Unknown word	Alternative word(s)	Unknown word	Alternative word(s)

Illustrations © 2010, Woody Fox.

Words and meanings

Two meanings in one

■ Read this poem. Underline the words with two meanings. There is one on each line of the poem.

Have you ever seen?
Have you ever seen a sheet on a river bed?
Or a single hair from a hammer's head?
Has the foot of a mountain any toes?
And is there a pair of garden hose?

Does the needle ever wink its eye?
Why doesn't the wing of a building fly?
Can you tickle the ribs of a parasol?
Or open the trunk of a tree at all?

Are the teeth of a rake ever going to bite?
Have the hands of a clock any left or right?
Can the garden plot be deep and dark?
And what is the sound of the birch's bark?

Anonymous

■ Choose at least four of the words and write the two meanings in the poem. Use a dictionary if you need to. The first one has been done for you.

bed	what you lie on at night to go to sleep	the bottom of a river

Name:

Words and meanings

Dictionary definitions

■ This is an extract from a dictionary. Can you work out the meaning of the Latin prefix **equi-** from the word definitions?

> **equidistant:** (adjective) being the same distance or having the same amount of space between.
> *The swimming pool is **equidistant** between the two schools so they both should be able to use it.*
> **equilateral:** (adjective) having all sides the same length.
> *An **equilateral** triangle is one with three sides the same length.*
> **equinox:** (noun) the two times a year when the lengths of day and night are the same.
> *Many people look forward to the spring **equinox** because they know that better weather is on the way.*
> **equivalent:** (adjective) the same in amount, value, or meaning.
> *One kilogram is **equivalent** to 1000 grams.*

equi- means _____

(Challenge!)

■ Look up **equator** in the dictionary. How does its meaning relate to the words above?
■ Look up the meanings of these prefixes in the dictionary: **micro-** and **hyper-**
■ Explain the meanings of these words to a partner.

| microcomputer | microfilm | microscope | hyperactive |
| hypercritical | hypermarket | | |

Old and new words

Objective

To explore how new words come into use in a language and others go out of use or change their meanings.

Background knowledge

All languages change, except those that have no living users, such as ancient Greek and Latin. New objects and ideas need new words. Often these new words are old words with new applications (*computer* originally meant a person who computes or performs calculations) or are formed from words already in existence (*online*, *on* and *line*, from the Latin *linea*, meaning thread or link). Words also cease to be in common use, such as for objects that no longer exist or have been superseded. Spoken language, particularly in informal usage, is especially subject to change, often from one generation to the next.

Activities

These activities explore words that are no longer in use for old technology, new words for new technology, and changing colloquial language.

● **Photocopiable page 44 'Old words for old things'**
Some items (and words) are not actually used any more (*gramophone*), while some are just perhaps old-fashioned but still in use (*cassette*). Discussion with adults of different ages will enable the children to work out which objects different generations remember using.

● **Photocopiable page 45 'New words for new things'**
Ask the children to write the original and the new technology-related definitions for the first set of words, such as *web* (threads spun by a spider to catch prey and

a computer network). Discuss the connection between the two meanings and why the word was chosen for its new context. For the compound words, ask the children to consider the meanings of the two parts and how they link to make the whole meaning.

● **Photocopiable page 46 'Changing language'**
Invite the children to talk to adults of different ages, to see how words come into and go out of fashion, such as *cool*, *wicked*, *sad* and *groovy*. Ask the children to write or perform dialogues, using words from different generations.

Further ideas

● **Old and new:** Use dictionaries and encyclopedias published at different times for a source of old and new words.

● **In other words:** Explore other areas of spoken language change, surveying different generations about words they use for food (*grub*) or money (*dosh*). Discuss geographical differences as well as generational.

● **Word roots:** Investigate the meanings of other words ending with '-phone' and '-graph', which might lead to other parts, such as 'tele-' and 'scope-'.

● **Language in literature:** Share extracts from books written or set at different times to explore language change, such as *The Railway Children* by E. Nesbit and *The Secret Garden* by Frances Hodgson Burnett.

● **ICT glossary:** Invite the children to compile a class glossary or dictionary for ICT. Lead to work on meanings of prefixes, such as 'inter-', 'intra-', 'mega-', 'hyper-' and 'micro-'.

What's on the CD-ROM

On the CD-ROM you will find:
● Printable versions of all three photocopiable pages.
● Answers to 'Old words for old things' and 'New words for new things'.
● Interactive version of 'New words for new things'.

Name:

Old and new words

Old words for old things

■ Sometimes words are not used anymore because the things they describe are not used anymore. Read this paragraph about the history of devices for recording and playing back sound.

The phonograph (from the Greek words **phone**, meaning sound, and **graphe**, meaning writing) was the first device for recording and playing sound. Sound was recorded on to a cylinder. It was invented by Thomas Edison in 1877. Emile Berliner developed the gramophone (from **grami**, meaning line, and **phone**, meaning sound) in 1887, which recorded sound on to a disc. At first, gramophones had to be wound up. Later they used electricity. The discs started to be called records and the machines were called record players. In the 1960s, stereophonic (stereo) hi-fi (hi-fidelity) systems were made that had a record player or turntable, and a cassette player. Cassettes contain two very small spools of tape, inside a plastic case. Compact discs (CDs) and CD players became available in 1982.

■ Write a list of words that you think are not used anymore.

_____

_____

_____

■ What do you listen to music on?

_____

_____

_____

■ Talk to older people. Find out which objects they remember and how they listened to music when they were younger.

Illustrations © 2010, Woody Fox.

Old and new words

New words for new things

◼ Kamal has written an email to his cousin Safiya to tell her about his new computer.

To: safiya.hassan@fastmail.com
Subject: New computer

Hi Safiya

I'm just writing to tell you about the new laptop my dad bought. It's much better than our old desktop computer because you can use it anywhere in the house and it doesn't crash all the time. You don't need a mouse because it has a touchpad instead but sometimes it's a bit tricky to point to the thing you want on a menu! We've got broadband connection so I can surf the web all day. I can download games and music really quickly. I found a funny screensaver on the internet and I've got a picture of the England football team as wallpaper. Dad says it's a good job we've got a firewall so we don't get spam or viruses. He says we might get a webcam next so that Granny can see us.

See you soon,
Kamal

◼ New inventions need new words. Sometimes new words are old words with new meanings. Sometimes new words are made by putting together two words or bits of words that already existed.

◼ Underline all the words in the email related to computers and technology.

◼ Write them in the boxes below and then find out more about their meanings. Try adding more words of your own.

Old words with new meanings	Two words put together
mouse	laptop

Name:

Changing language

This is part of a telephone call between Stacey and her friend Zoe.

(Z): Yeah it was really cool.

(Z): And did you see the geek dancing in the corner?

(S): Hi Zoe. It's Stacey. It was a wicked party yesterday wasn't it?

(S): But the games were a bit sad weren't they?

■ Write in the boxes the words that Stacey and Zoe use to describe things that are good and things that are not good. Are they words that you would use?

■ Add more words that you might use.

■ Talk to as many grown-ups as you can to find out the words they use for **good** and **not good** and the words they used when they were young.

Questions to think about:
• Which words do you think are not used anymore?
• Which words are used now that were not used in the past?
• Which words are in the dictionary? Which words have changed their meaning?

Good things	Not good things
wicked	

PHOTOCOPIABLE

Illustrations © 2010, Woody Fox.

Different meanings

Objective

To explore literal and metaphorical meanings of words and phrases.

Background knowledge

In this section the children will learn that words can have different meanings and that they do not always mean what they say. A kenning is a shortened metaphor, originally used in Anglo-Saxon and Norse poetry, where an object is described in a two-word phrase, such as *whale-road* for *sea*. English abounds with expressions that cannot be determined by reference to a dictionary. Some are so commonly used that we tend to forget that they are metaphorical.

Activities

The children use a kenning to explore different ways of describing familiar things, match literal to metaphorical meanings of phrases and explore double meanings in a poem.

● **Photocopiable page 48 'Squirrel'**
Read the poem to the children, without the title or last line, and ask them to guess what is being described. Discuss the form of the poem: two-word lines, noun and verb. Use shared writing to model how to turn an idea into a two-word phrase. Poems do not need to rhyme, although some of the children will enjoy this challenge.

● **Photocopiable page 49 'I don't mean what I say'**
Use one or two examples to illustrate the connection between the literal and the metaphorical meanings. Encourage the children to pay close attention to the literal meanings of the words in the phrase. Challenge them to write a short story using as many of the phrases (and others) as possible. Discuss the fact that using too many of these phrases will make their writing sound clichéd.

● **Photocopiable page 50 'More than one meaning'**
Ensure that there is plenty of discussion about meanings of expressions, such as *shop-lifter*, helping the children to appreciate the humour of the poet's images. Work in pairs or small groups, with adult support or dictionaries as appropriate, to encourage talk about meanings and the ways in which the humour is created. Add lines to the poem as a shared writing activity.

Further ideas

● **Web:** Websites such as www.poetryarchive.org and www.kidsonthenet.com contain examples of kennings, including those written by children.
● **More kennings:** Let the children write kennings about other subjects or members of their family, or write about a class member for others to guess.
● **Collecting phrases:** Collect other metaphorical phrases from shared and personal reading and from other sources, such as television and radio. Make a display of illustrations. Research the origins of different phrases.
● **Homonym jokes:** Collect and define other homonyms. Share jokes based on homonyms and discuss the double meanings. For example: *What did the triangle say to the circle? You're so pointless* and *Why can't Cinderella be in the football team? Because she always runs away from the ball.*

What's on the CD-ROM

On the CD-ROM you will find:
● Printable versions of all three photocopiable pages.
● Answers to 'I don't mean what I say' and 'More than one meaning'.
● Interactive version of 'I don't mean what I say'.

Name:

Different meanings

Squirrel

- ■ Notice how each line in the poem uses just two words to describe a squirrel.
- ■ Choose an animal and write a list of all the things you know about it. Think about what it looks like, sounds like, feels like and the things it does.
- ■ Use your ideas to write a poem.

Squirrel

Woodland racer
Acorn chaser
Tree shaker
Acorn taker
Nut cracker
Acorn snacker
Sky rider
Acorn hider
Winter snoozer
Acorn loser
Spring reminder
Acorn finder:
One grey squirrel.

Celia Warren

My animal _____

_____

_____

_____

_____

_____

_____

_____

Poem © 2000, Celia Warren; Illustrations © 2010, Woody Fox.

Different meanings

I don't mean what I say

■ Match these phrases to their metaphorical meanings. The first one has been done for you. Write the phrase with its meaning in your book.

■ Draw pictures to illustrate the literal meaning of each phrase.

It's raining cats and dogs.	She revealed a secret.
He has turned over a new leaf.	He can't make a decision.
She's burning the candle at both ends.	It's pouring with rain.
We'll cross that bridge when we come to it.	I suspect something is wrong.
She let the cat out of the bag.	I'm feeling a bit ill.
He's sitting on the fence.	He has made a fresh start.
I can smell a rat.	He thinks he's cleverer or more important than he really is.
He's leading you up the garden path.	She's working very hard, day and night.
I'm feeling a bit under the weather.	He's trying to fool you.
He's too big for his boots.	We'll deal with that problem when we need to.

Name:

Different meanings

More than one meaning

■   This poem plays with meanings of common expressions. Each couplet contains an expression where the words could have more than one meaning.

On and on...

Is a well-wisher
    someone
who wishes at a well?

Is a bad-speller
    one
who casts a wicked spell?

Is a shop-lifter
    a giant
who goes around lifting shops?

Is a popsinger
    someone
who sings and then pops?

Is a pot-holer
    a gunman
who shoots holes in pots?

Does a baby-sitter
    really
sit on tiny tots?

Is a light bulb
    a bulb
that is light as a feather?

Does an opera buff
    sing
in the altogether?

Does a pony trap
    trap
ponies going to the fair?

Is fire-hose
    stockings
that fireman wear?

Is a scratch team
    so itchy
it scratches?

When a bricklayer
    lays a brick
what hatches?

Is a sick bed
    a bed
that is feeling unwell?

Is a crime wave
    a criminal's
wave of farewell?

Is a bent copper
    a policeman
who has gone round the bend?

Is the bottom line
    the line
on your bottom?

THE END
    Roger McGough

■   In your book or on paper choose four of the expressions and write down what each one means.

■   In each expression decide which word could have two meanings and write down the meanings. Use a dictionary if you need to. Set it out like this:

Expression	Meaning	Word with two meanings	First meaning	Second meaning
well-wisher	someone who wants someone else to have good luck	well	healthy or fortunate	a hole in the ground that you can get water from

PHOTOCOPIABLE   **SCHOLASTIC**
www.scholastic.co.uk

Poem © 1993, Roger McGough.

Assessment

The following grid shows the main objectives and activities covered in this chapter. You can use the grid to locate activities that cover a particular focus that you are keen to monitor.

Objective	Page	Activity title
To collect and explore words related to particular contexts or topics.	36 37 38	Our school library Tools of the trade What do I do?
To use context to work out meanings of unfamiliar words.	40 41 42	Meanings in context Two meanings in one Dictionary definitions
To use dictionaries to find word meanings, definitions and origins.	40 41 42	Meanings in context Two meanings in one Dictionary definitions
To explore how new words come into use in a language and others go out of use or change their meanings.	44 45 46	Old words for old things New words for new things Changing language
To explore literal and metaphorical meanings of words and phrases.	48 49 50	Squirrel I don't mean what I say More than one meaning

Observation and record keeping

Assessment should track the children's development in both knowledge and skills. You could record the children's areas of strength and targets for development in the following areas:
- knowledge of vocabulary related to familiar topics
- ability to recognise links in families of words
- ability to generate words by association with a given context or topic

- ability to use context to work out meanings of unfamiliar words
- understanding that a dictionary can be used to find meanings and origins of words
- knowledge that language changes
- developing understanding of the ways in which it changes and the reasons for change
- understanding of the word *homonym*
- understanding that words and phrases are not always used literally
- developing the ability to use vocabulary for effect.

Assessment activity

- **What you need**
Photocopiable page 52 'Working out meanings', appropriate dictionaries.
- **What to do**
The activity assesses the children's ability to make connections in meaning between words with the same parts and to differentiate the two meanings of a homonym. Carry out the activity in small groups to allow observation of the children's approaches and use of dictionaries. Encourage the children to work out meanings from the clues given and check afterwards in a dictionary.

Differentiation

- For less confident learners, carry out the activity orally emphasising the relevant parts of words. Use further examples or pictures to give additional support.
- Challenge more confident learners to suggest other words ending with *proof* and use dictionaries to find words with the prefix 'sub-', putting them in sentences to illustrate their meaning.

Further learning

- **Affixes:** Take every opportunity to draw attention to words with common roots or affixes, demonstrating how they give clues to meaning.
- **Shared reading:** Use shared reading to model how to determine the meaning of an unfamiliar word.
- **Homonym word class:** Find homonyms that belong to different word classes, such as *note*: a noun (short letter or musical sound) or verb (to spot something or jot something).

Name:

Working out meanings

Waterproof means not letting water through or into something.
A waterproof coat keeps you dry.

■ Find a word to fit in these sentences.

A _____ door does not let fire through.

A _____ lid cannot be opened by a child.

A **submarine** is a vessel that can go under the sea.
Sub means under and **marine** means the sea.

■ What do these words mean?

subtitle _____

subzero _____

■ Tick the correct meaning of the homonyms in these sentences.

I am going to **train** every day for Saturday's match.

a form of transport
that runs on rails ☐   practise hard ☐

Jack wrote a **note** to his friend Rosie.

a short letter ☐   a musical sound ☐

Cinderella met Prince Charming at the **ball**.

a round
bouncy toy ☐   a dance with
lots of people ☐

Word of the week

The Word of the week pages provide information on one word linked to each section in the chapter. Each word is described in some of the following categories: word definition, word origin, word family, alternative words, fascinating facts and activities. Not all categories are relevant to every word.

You can use the words as a focus to support your work on the different sections of the chapter. For example, you could create a display around it. The information is a starting point for a word focus. The words could form part of your classroom living word bank.

You could also use the word of the week as a springboard to inspire children to think about or research fascinating facts about words, find interesting quotations and to encourage them to use dictionaries and thesauruses.

Library

- **Word definition:** A noun meaning a collection of books.
- **Word origin:** From the Latin *liber* (pronounced with long i), meaning to peel.
- **Word family:** Noun: *librarian*.
- **Alternative words:** Book room, reference centre, resource centre.
- **Fascinating facts:** The soft inner bark of trees, on which early manuscripts were written, was peeled from the tree. *Liber* then became the word for paper, and then *libra* (*book*). A *librarium* was a bookcase. *Library* shares its origin with the word *leaf*, hence a book page or to turn over the pages of a book.

> Linked section: Words in a context, page 35

- **Activities:** Explore meanings of words such as *leaflet*, and phrases such as *turning over a new leaf* (see 'Different meanings' on page 47). In the sense that a library is a collection of books, the children can label different collections in the classroom, such as *our poetry/science/non-fiction library*. Allocate librarians to each collection.

Hyper

- **Word definition:** A prefix meaning excessively; also colloquial adjective meaning over-excited or overactive.
- **Word origin:** From the Greek originally meaning over, and hence excess or exaggeration.
- **Word family:** Noun: *hype*; verb: *hyped up*.
- **Alternative words:** Excitable, frenzied, highly strung, hot-headed, manic, overactive, overexcited, restless, unbalanced.

> Linked section: Words and meanings, page 39

- **Fascinating facts:** 'Hyper-' and 'super-' can be used in similar ways, with 'hyper-' meaning even more so. *Super* is a Latin word meaning above and as a prefix is used to mean both physically above (*superimpose*, *superstructure*) and more figuratively, something or someone that exceeds customary norms (*superman*, *supercomputer*). *Super* has been used as a standalone word for a long time, whereas *hyper* is a more recent coinage and is still considered very colloquial.
- **Activities:** Let the children have fun adding the prefixes 'super-' and 'hyper-' to words and judging their effect, such as *superskilful* and *hyperskilful*; *supercold* and *hypercold*; *superstar* and *hyperstar*. Explore the meaning and uses of the word *hype* (to publicise or promote, especially by extravagant, inflated or misleading claims), as in *the hype surrounding the film launch*.

Groovy

- **Word definition:** An adjective meaning excellent or fashionable.
- **Word origin:** Probably from the Dutch *groef*, meaning furrow.
- **Word family:** Noun: *groove, groover.*
- **Alternative words (colloquial):** Cool, excellent, fantastic, fashionable, great, hip, terrific, trendy.
- **Fascinating facts:** Although well known as a hippie word from the 1960s, *groovy* was first used in the 1930s, where American jazz musicians were described as *being in the groove*. It is thought that this refers to the newly available gramophone records (see 'Old words for old things' on page 44) where a needle travelled in a continuous spiral channel called a groove. *Groovy* was then used to describe anything particularly good. The word was revived in the 1960s (including in the song *Feelin' Groovy* by Simon and Garfunkel), but is now used only by the generation who were young then or in a deliberately retro way. Interestingly, the word *cool*, which dates from the same period, has remained a 'cool' word to use.
- **Activities:** Get the children using groovy as often as possible: *This is a really groovy science experiment/maths problem/spelling test.* Challenge the children to use it in a literal sense: *The football pitch/hall floor is really groovy.*

> **Linked section:**
> Old and new words,
> page 43

Under the weather

- **Phrase definition:** An idiom used to describe feeling rather ill.
- **Phrase origin:** It probably refers to the fact that people's physical and mental state can reflect the weather. When it is cold and dark people can feel tired and miserable.
- **Phrase family:** Feeling rough, off colour, on my last legs, like death warmed up.
- **Alternative words:** Poorly, ill, sick, unhealthy, unwell.
- **Fascinating facts:** Alternatively it is possible that the phrase has a maritime origin: when sailors were sick they would rest below deck and be literally *under the weather* or *under the weather deck*, the most exposed deck on the ship.
- **Activities:** As part of a geography topic on the weather, ask the children to research other expressions or idioms that use weather images. There are a number of useful websites, such as www.usingenglish.com. For example, *make heavy weather of*, *the calm before the storm, chasing rainbows, come rain or shine, a fair-weather friend, know which way the wind blows, snowed under* (with work), *it's a breeze*. Extend this to weather folklore, such as *Red sky at night, shepherd's delight, Red sky in the morning, shepherd's warning* (see www.weatherwizkids.com).

> **Linked section:**
> Different meanings,
> page 47

Fun with words

· ·

Use these activities to support the vocabulary work in this chapter. They could be used as starter or plenary activities.

Lunchtime
● Play word association. Put the children in groups and give a starter word, such as *lunchtime*. Each person in turn has to give the first word that comes to mind connected with the previous word. The children can challenge any contribution that they do not think is connected. If the challenged child can explain the connection, they gain a point, otherwise the challenger wins a point.

What's my line?
● Play this game with the children in small groups or pairs. Each pair or group is given, or can choose, an occupation (hairdresser, footballer, post-person), without other groups knowing what it is. The children have to write a list of words connected with that occupation for the others to guess what it is.

Homonym sentences
● Write a homonym on the board. Award points to the quickest group or pair to come up with two different definitions or two sentences illustrating the meaning.

Homonym illustrations
● Write homonyms on cards. Let each pair or group draw two pictures to illustrate the two meanings for others to guess.

Categories
● Prepare cards with words connected with different topics, such as *sports*, *animals* and *transport* (one word per card). Mix them up and give them to the children to sort into groups and then provide a 'title' for each group. This can be varied by providing cards that could all fall into one category, such as *animals*, but have to be sorted using more refined criteria, such as *farm animals* or *pets*.

Draw it!
● Play this game with well-known expressions written on cards, such as *spring-cleaning* or *pulling a face*. Let the children work in groups, taking turns to choose a card and draw the literal meaning for others to guess. Award points to guessers if they are right, or the drawer if not. (*Paying through the nose and other English expressions* by Andrew Niccol is an excellent resource. It is no longer in print, but available secondhand.)

Proverbs
● Explore non-literal meanings further in proverbs, such as *Too many cooks spoil the broth*. Ask the children to prepare two role plays, one for the literal meaning of the proverb and one for a contemporary situation in which it might apply.

Chapter 3
Grammar

Introduction

This chapter focuses on developing different types of vocabulary for specific purposes. The activities can be used alongside work on grammar to reinforce the function of adjectives, adverbs, verbs and connectives (including conjunctions), with an emphasis on extending the range of words used by the children in a variety of contexts. The children will also begin to make conscious vocabulary choices in speech and writing according to the purpose and audience, becoming aware of the difference between formal and informal contexts.

In this chapter

Adjectives and adverbs page 58	To extend knowledge of appropriate and powerful adjectives.
Verbs page 62	To extend the range of verbs used for particular contexts.
Formal and informal language page 66	To understand that vocabulary choices vary according to purpose and audience. To acquire a range of vocabulary for formal and informal occasions.
Conjunctions and connectives page 70	To extend the range of conjunctions and time connectives used to link clauses and sentences.
Assessment page 74	Activities and ideas to assess the ability to use a range of appropriate adjectives, verbs, conjunctions and connectives.

Poster notes

Conjunctions (page 57)
The poster illustrates the function of conjunctions in joining two sentences. It can be used as an introduction to photocopiable page 71 'Mystery story' and to explore the effect of substituting different conjunctions in sentences and of changing the order of the starting sentences. As the children come across more examples of conjunctions and sentences, they can add these.

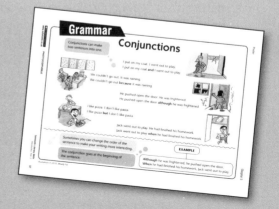

Grammar

Conjunctions

Conjunctions can make two sentences into one.

I put on my coat. I went out to play.
I put on my coat **and** I went out to play.

We couldn't go out. It was raining.
We couldn't go out **because** it was raining.

He pushed open the door. He was frightened.
He pushed open the door **although** he was frightened.

I like pizza. I don't like pasta.
I like pizza **but** I don't like pasta.

Jack went out to play. He had finished his homework.
Jack went out to play **when** he had finished his homework.

Sometimes you can change the order of the sentence to make your writing more interesting.

The conjunction goes at the beginning of the sentence.

EXAMPLE

Although he was frightened, he pushed open the door.
When he had finished his homework, Jack went out to play.

Illustrations © 2010, Woody Fox.

Adjectives and adverbs

Objective

To extend knowledge of appropriate and powerful adjectives.

Background knowledge

These activities can be used alongside grammar tasks to reinforce word classes and extend vocabulary. Adjectives (to modify nouns) and adverbs (most commonly to modify verbs) are used in all types of writing for precise description and to add interest for the reader. Writing with no adjectives or adverbs can be flat and not very engaging, although overuse can be intrusive. Writers choose particular words to create their desired effect on the reader.

Activities

These activities give the children a vocabulary to describe feelings, an important aspect of personal and social education, as well as illustrating the power of adjectives and adverbs, encouraging the children to select appropriate and varied vocabulary.

● **Photocopiable page 59 'How are you feeling?'**
Introduce the activity by asking the children to show you a bored, angry or excited face. Let them work in pairs on the activity, encouraging them to describe to a partner an occasion when they have experienced particular feelings. Ideas for poetry can be as exaggerated as the children want.

● **Photocopiable page 60 'Film review'**
Encourage the children to use dictionaries to check meanings of unknown adjectives to extend their vocabulary. Note that the final two adjectives require a different approach, since they are positive. Evaluate the children's reports in the plenary. Extend this by

discussing the appropriateness of particular adjectives for particular occasions, noting that some are quite general, such as *marvellous*, while others relate to more specific contexts, such as *attractive*. Invite the children to write their own film reviews.

● **Photocopiable page 61 'Football report'**
Read the report without adverbs to the children before they do the activity, noting the difference once adverbs are added. The children may make different choices, which can be evaluated. Ask the children to read out their finished reports, making them sound as exciting as possible.

Further ideas

● **Once more with feeling:** Ask the children to find synonyms and antonyms for feelings words and evaluate their effects for particular contexts. Ask the children to make illustrated feelings posters for the classroom and devise role plays to illustrate particular feelings for others to guess.

● **Adjectives to adverbs:** Explore the way in which many adverbs are formed by adding '-ly' to adjectives. Put adjectives and their corresponding adverbs into sentences to illustrate their use. Write adverb poems, where the adverb is the first word of each line: *Slowly…, Silently…, Suddenly…*

● **Collecting descriptive words:** Use shared and personal reading and writing to collect and celebrate effective adjectives and adverbs. Classify them into adjectives for size, colour, mood, speed and so on.

What's on the CD-ROM

On the CD-ROM you will find:
● Printable versions of all three photocopiable pages.
● Answers to 'How are you feeling?'.
● Interactive versions of 'How are you feeling?' and 'Film review'.

Adjectives and adverbs

How are you feeling?

■ Match each picture to a feeling. The first one has been done for you.

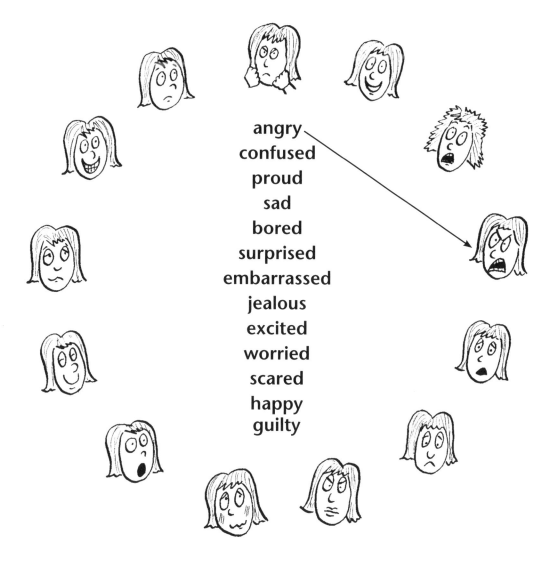

angry
confused
proud
sad
bored
surprised
embarrassed
jealous
excited
worried
scared
happy
guilty

■ Choose a feeling and write a poem about it. Here is one to start you off.

I was so bored …
…I would rather have watched paint dry.
I was so bored …
…the whole football team would fit in my yawns.
I was so bored …
…I'd even clean the school hall floor with a toothbrush.

Name:

Adjectives and adverbs

Film review

■ Read the review of the film below. The reviewer clearly did not enjoy this film. Notice how the negative adjectives make the review sound negative.

■ You really liked the film, however, so you need to rewrite the review below by changing the adjectives in bold to make it sound positive. You could use some of the words from the box or choose your own.

Review of new release,

The Final Curtain

by our film correspondent, Louise Lovelace

The **unattractive** Kerry Kingley stars in this **boring** new movie. The plot is **unbelievable** and **dull**. The film opens with an **uninspiring** and **clumsy** car chase. The **unconvincing** and **disagreeable** hero, played by Craig Crossland uncovers a plot by an **amateurish** villain, Judas Judge, to take over the world. The **tedious** story unfolds in further **slow-moving** events. The performances by the main characters are **lacklustre** and the special effects are **routine** and **ridiculous**. The ending is **disappointing** and **predictable**. Overall this is a **dreary, monotonous** film and I felt **relieved** and **delighted** when it had finished.

thrilling	exhilarating	electrifying	sensational	beautiful
charming	breathtaking	appealing	fascinating	
good-looking	exciting	marvellous	attractive	dynamic
slick	polished	superb	remarkable	astonishing	clever

_____

_____

_____

_____

_____

_____

Adjectives and adverbs

Football report

■ Read this extract from a report of a football match.

■ Choose an appropriate adverb to fill each gap. Use the adverbs in the box below or choose your own. Use a different adverb each time. Then read your rewritten report. Notice how much more exciting it sounds.

Southam United were defending _____

as James _____ bent a corner into the box.

Mark _____ headed the ball clear to Henry who

_____ brought it under control and _____

chipped it wide to Jack. Jack advanced _____ down the left

and _____ beat three players. He _____

flicked the ball to Muhammed who _____ cut back on to

his right foot. Muhammed _____ whipped a cross into the

box towards Dan who _____ controlled the ball before

_____ volleying it past the _____

stretching keeper.

delicately	bravely	elegantly	confidently	cleverly
quickly	menacingly	spectacularly	dangerously	
desperately	accurately	brilliantly	frantically	

_____

_____

_____

_____

_____

Verbs

Objective

To extend the range of verbs used for particular contexts.

Background knowledge

This section focuses on action verbs, but, if linked to work on grammar, a more extended notion of verb will be needed, including the verb *to be*. Since all true sentences contain at least one verb, they are very important in writing. If selected carefully, they make all types of writing more interesting and more precise. Verbs for different ways of moving will be particularly valuable in story writing, to avoid repetition of *went*, for example. Imperative verbs are an essential element of instructions. Different types of instructions have particular fields of imperatives that the children should be aware of.

Activities

The children learn a wide range of verbs for moving, explore a variety of other verbs and investigate different types of imperatives for different types of instructions.

● **Photocopiable page 63 'Action verbs'**
Do this activity in the hall or playground. Demonstrate, or ask the children to demonstrate, the meaning of some of the more unusual verbs. Let the children use dictionaries to check other words and give each partner a copy of all the words as a prompt.

● **Photocopiable page 64 'Doing things'**
Share the poem as a class, noting the humour in the 'trivial' nature of the things the poet describes. Focus on the '-ing' verbs at the beginning of each line. Discuss the other verbs, including auxiliaries. Use shared writing to begin a new poem, using the children's ideas. Some children may require adult support to compose a group poem, to then read aloud or dramatise.

● **Photocopiable page 65 'Bossy verbs'**
Let the children initially use verbs, nouns and adjectives to decide on the type of instruction. Then invite them to focus on the imperatives. Show that some imperatives could be used in different types of instructions, such as *cross* and *pass* (directions or game). Encourage the children to make posters of useful imperatives for particular types of instructions.

Further ideas

● **Using verbs in writing:** Encourage the children to use a range of action verbs in their writing. Celebrate and display particularly appropriate and adventurous vocabulary.
● **Sports verbs:** Compile a list of games and sports. Ask each pair or group to take one activity and generate a list of related verbs. For example, *rounders* might generate *throw*, *hit*, *run*, *catch*, *strike*, *bat*, *bowl* and *field*.
● **Missing verbs:** Cover all the verbs in an extract from a relevant text and ask the children to discuss possibilities for filling in the gaps. Evaluate the suggestions against the original, noting that the intention is not to guess the right answer.
● **Random verbs:** As a variation, ask the children to generate a list of verbs to insert before seeing the text. While creating amusing results, it also highlights the importance of careful selection of vocabulary.

What's on the CD-ROM

On the CD-ROM you will find:
● Printable versions of all three photocopiable pages.
● Answers to 'Doing things' and 'Bossy verbs'.
● Interactive version of 'Bossy verbs'.

Verbs

Action verbs

■ Work with a partner. Read the words on the cards and check that you know what they mean. Use a dictionary if you need to.

■ Cut out the cards and put them in a pile face down. Take turns to take a card and move in the manner suggested by the word. Can your partner guess what the word is?

stalk	wander	dash	scramble
stamp	shuffle	stagger	creep
totter	hobble	swagger	amble
sneak	waddle	march	plod
prance	stride	saunter	strut

Name:

Verbs

Doing things

■ Underline the verb in each line of the poem below.

Things I have been doing lately

Things I have been doing lately:
Pretending to go mad
Eating my own cheeks from the inside
Growing taller
Keeping a secret
Keeping a worm in a jar
Keeping a good dream going
Picking a scab on my elbow
Rolling the cat up in a rug
Blowing bubbles in my spit
Making myself dizzy
Holding my breath
Pressing my eyeballs so that I become temporarily blind
Being very nearly ten
Practising my signature …
Saving the best till last.

Allan Ahlberg

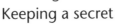

■ Write a list of things you have been doing, in your book or on a piece of paper. Start with just a list of verbs, such as **thinking, jumping, remembering** and **sleeping**.

■ Turn each idea into a line of a poem, like Allan Ahlberg's.

_____

_____

_____

_____

Poem © 1991, Allan Ahlberg; illustrations © 2010, Woody Fox.

Verbs

Bossy verbs

■ These are all extracts from different types of instructions. What kind of instructions are they? How do you know? Highlight the imperative (bossy) verbs. The first one has been done for you.

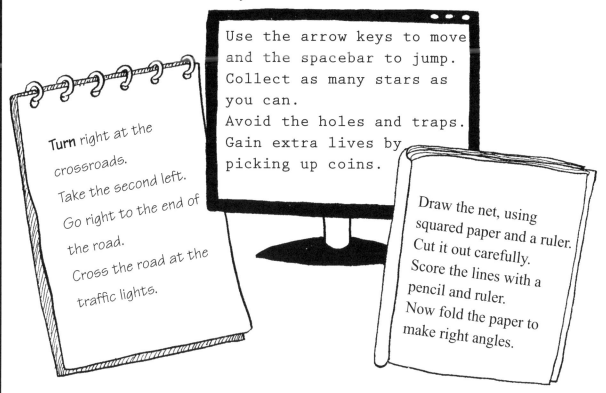

Turn right at the crossroads.
Take the second left.
Go right to the end of the road.
Cross the road at the traffic lights.

Use the arrow keys to move and the spacebar to jump.
Collect as many stars as you can.
Avoid the holes and traps.
Gain extra lives by picking up coins.

Draw the net, using squared paper and a ruler.
Cut it out carefully.
Score the lines with a pencil and ruler.
Now fold the paper to make right angles.

■ These are mixed up imperatives. Sort them into their correct sets. Some have been done for you already.

play   turn   bend   continue   fold   take   move   go
pass   colour   walk   collect   save   cut   paint
rescue   load   tear   start   follow   avoid
draw   cross   defeat   stick

Game playing	Directions	Craft
play	turn	fold

Illustrations © 2010, Woody Fox.

Formal and informal language

Objectives

To understand that vocabulary choices vary according to purpose and audience. To acquire a range of vocabulary for formal and informal occasions.

Background knowledge

Most people speak informal English, which is relaxed about grammar and vocabulary. Informal writing reflects this relaxation. Newspaper articles are often written informally, and informal language is used when writing to friends. Formal English is, for the most part, a written language. It is used in textbooks, academic or technical works, and for official letters. It tends to be impersonal and precise, using a more specialised and complex vocabulary. Instant messaging and text messaging are at the extreme end of informal writing and often reflect spoken language. Children become aware quite early of the need to use spoken language differently in different situations. This section emphasises an awareness of appropriate uses of language to suit the audience, purpose and context.

Activities

A spoken language transcript, a non-fiction report and electronic instant messaging demonstrate the differences between formal and informal language, encouraging the children to make conscious choices in both speech and writing.

● **Photocopiable page 67 'Kids' TV'**
Ask the children to read the dialogue aloud in pairs. Model a rewrite of the first sentence and discuss differences of vocabulary and grammar. Invite the children to evaluate each other's dialogues. Discuss the appropriateness of the formal and informal versions. The informal version may be more lively, but will it be taken seriously?

● **Photocopiable page 68 'Non-fiction reports'**
Read the first sentence aloud, first using the less formal and then the more formal option. Discuss the effect of the alternatives (more impersonal and technical perhaps). Let the children use a thesaurus to find alternatives for the bold words and evaluate the different choices.

● **Photocopiable page 69 'Instant messaging'**
Pair any children who are unfamiliar with instant messaging with an expert. Discuss and list features of the language used in this context (developed to keep the number of characters to a minimum, like text messaging). Ask the children to rewrite the conversation using informal language. As a plenary, consider the inappropriateness of formal words and phrases in this context.

Further ideas

● **Shared reading:** Use shared text opportunities to highlight formal and informal language in a range of different texts. For example, the children might note that in a story the narrative is probably written more formally than the dialogue.

● **Colloquial language:** Explore other informal words and phrases and find more formal alternatives, such as *I'm all for…*, *I'm dead against…*, *I'm up for it*. Compile a class glossary of colloquialisms and instant messaging abbreviations.

● **Role play:** Set up role-play contexts with different audiences. For example, ask the children to describe an incident in the playground to a friend and to the headteacher. Discuss appropriate vocabulary choices.

What's on the CD-ROM

On the CD-ROM you will find:
● Printable versions of all three photocopiable pages.
● Answers to all three photocopiable pages.
● Interactive version of 'Non-fiction reports'.

Kids' TV

■   Bob and Bethany had an idea for a new children's television show. They went to the television company, Kids' TV, to try to persuade them to use their idea. Below is the script of what they said to the producer and her assistant.

■   Bob and Bethany use a lot of informal language. Rewrite their pitch, in your book or on another piece of paper, using more formal language.

Bob: Hi there, we're here today to pitch our idea for a fab new TV show for kids.

Bethany: Yeah, we reckon we've got a sure-fire winner here.

Bob: So, what's it all about? Well, first off we've got some wacky characters that kids are gonna love.

Bethany: Yep, and there'll be some crazy cartoons to hook them in.

Bob: There's stacks of competitions and prizes up for grabs.

Bethany: And loads of wild games and loony goings-on.

Bob: But the best thing of all is that it's all about healthy living.

Bethany: Yeah, kids are gonna want to be like their fave characters and eat heaps of healthy grub and get out there working out and keeping fit.

Bob and Bethany: So, that's it. What do you think guys?

Name:

Non-fiction reports

■ Non-fiction reports usually use formal language. Read this report about the River Thames and choose the more formal word or phrase in each case.

The River Thames

During the first half of the 20th century the **state/quality** of the water in the River Thames **declined/fell**. A report in the 1950s **stated/said** that it was the **most polluted/dirtiest** river in England. A **real try/ determined effort** was made from 1960 onwards to **decontaminate/ clean up** the Thames in London, with the **result/upshot** that it is now one of the cleanest rivers in the world.

The water **looks/appears** rather **mucky/murky**, but now **contains/ has** over 115 different **species/kinds** of fish and they **feed/support** a growing **number/population** of birds **such as/like** herons and cormorants. Otters have been **seen/sighted** in some **places/locations**, and salmon now swim up the Thames to **lay eggs/spawn** – a sure **indicator/sign** of how clean the river has become, as wild salmon are **fussy/particular** about their **surroundings/environment**.

Illustrations © 2010, Woody Fox.

Formal and informal language

Instant messaging

■ David and Sanjit often chat on an instant messenger site. They use lots of abbreviations and quick spelling and often leave words out.

■ Rewrite their conversation, with correct spelling, adding missing words to make full sentences and punctuation where needed.

David:	hi m8, how r u?
Sanjit:	yeh ok thx
David:	wot u up 2 2moro?
Sanjit:	nuthin mch, wanna do sumthin, u got ne ideas?
David:	wot bout goin 2 movies…
Sanjit:	yeh def, dat new Bond films out aint it?
David:	yeh we cud go c dat I spose…
Sanjit:	wkd! time?
David:	bout 7ish…?
Sanjit:	gr8, wel up 4 it! LOL
David:	k cool, btw… can ur dad give us a lift?
Sanjit:	no prob m8, txt u wen leavin
David:	cool, g2g l8r
Sanjit:	yeah, cu

_____

_____

_____

_____

Illustrations © 2010, Woody Fox.

Conjunctions and connectives

Objective

To extend the range of conjunctions and time connectives used to link clauses and sentences.

Background knowledge

Connectives are a large class of words and phrases used to join words, phrases and clauses within sentences and to link sentences within texts. They can be conjunctions or connecting adverbs (or adverbial phrases). Conjunctions are only used within sentences to join words, phrases and clauses. They include: *and*, *but*, *or*, *so* (coordinating conjunctions, forming compound sentences); and *when*, *because*, *although*, *until*, *if* (subordinating conjunctions, forming complex sentences). Connecting adverbs are used to link sentences to maintain cohesion within texts. They include *however*, *meanwhile*, *therefore* and *on the other hand*.

Activities

The children add a range of conjunctions to a story opener and use appropriate time connectives in a recount and a set of instructions.

● **Photocopiable page 71 'Mystery story'**
Encourage the children to work in pairs, reading aloud as they insert conjunctions to check for grammatical sense and meaning. Note the position of the conjunction in the sentence (*Now that*) *she had come this far, she had to go on*. This builds suspense by leaving the key information till last. Use the plenary to discuss whether different conjunctions could fit in particular gaps. Extend the activity by splitting the text into simple sentences (some words will need to change) and evaluating the effect. Explore where the order of the two clauses could be swapped and the effect of this.

● **Photocopiable page 72 'Time connectives for stories'**
Ensure the children are familiar with the story. Use shared writing to add two or three sentences to the letter on the sheet, using different connectives. Invite the children to read their letters to the rest of the class, who should put up their hands every time they hear a connective. Give rewards for using and recognising connectives not listed on the sheet.

● **Photocopiable page 73 'How to make a cup of tea'**
Sequence the images as a class. Compose instructions orally and model one or two before the children write them down, discussing imperatives if necessary. Keep the focus on the selection of appropriate connectives. Discuss words such as *while* if necessary. Model, for example, *While the kettle is boiling, get a cup*.

Further ideas

● **Collect connectives:** Make class or individual collections of connectives from reading and writing and classify them into conjunctions and other connectives. Further classify, if appropriate, into connectives for different purposes, such as time (*before*, *next*), addition (*moreover*, *also*, *as well*), emphasis (*especially*, *above all*, *indeed*), and cause and effect (*because*, *therefore*, *so*).

● **Combining sentences:** Provide clauses or sentences and conjunctions on cards. Ask the children to join two clauses or sentences randomly with conjunctions and evaluate the grammatical and real-world sense of the results.

 What's on the CD-ROM

On the CD-ROM you will find:
● Printable versions of all three photocopiable pages.
● Answers to 'Mystery story'.
● Interactive versions of 'Mystery story' and 'How to make a cup of tea'.

Conjunctions and connectives

Mystery story

■ We use conjunctions to link words or parts of sentences together. Choose a conjunction from the box below to fill the gaps in this story opening.

What happened next?

Anya left her friend's house

_____ started to walk

home. It was beginning to get dark

_____ it was only half past four.

She whistled to herself _____

she scuffed her feet in the dry leaves.

She was passing the derelict church

_____ she heard a sound.

Was that someone crying _____

was it just the wind? Anya slowly pushed

open the creaky gate _____ looking nervously around. Suddenly

she shivered _____ someone was behind her. She wanted to run

_____ she could see nobody _____ she crept up

the path towards the decaying church door. She stopped for a moment to listen

_____ stepping into the shadow of the porch. _____

she had come this far, she had to go on. Suddenly she heard it again. The cry sent

shivers down her spine _____ it seemed to be calling her. Anya put

her hand on the huge rusty handle and pushed…

but	so	as if	as	and	now that
yet	before	although	when		
	while	or			

Illustrations © 2010, Woody Fox.

Name:

Conjunctions and connectives

Time connectives for stories

■ These words and phrases are connectives. They can be used to link sentences. They all show how time passes in a story. Can you add any more useful time connectives?

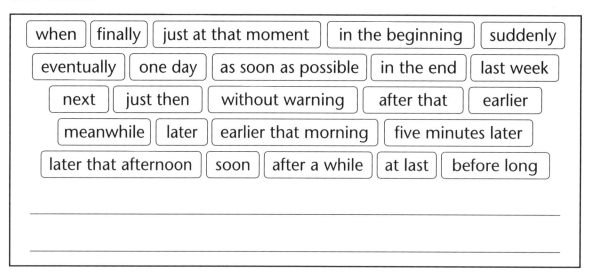

when	finally	just at that moment	in the beginning	suddenly
eventually	one day	as soon as possible	in the end	last week
next	just then	without warning	after that	earlier
meanwhile	later	earlier that morning	five minutes later
later that afternoon	soon	after a while	at last	before long

_____

_____

■ Imagine you are the oldest and most sensible of the three little pigs (you built your house with bricks). On a separate piece of paper, write a letter to your mother describing your adventures since you left home. Use time connectives to link your recount together. Begin your letter like this:

Patrick Pig
The Brick House
Cloverville

Dear Mother

After we left home, we walked a long way. Eventually we met a man carrying some straw. Percy decided to build a house as soon as possible and before long he had a cosy little straw house.

PHOTOCOPIABLE ■SCHOLASTIC
www.scholastic.co.uk

Conjunctions and connectives

How to make a cup of tea

■ These pictures show how to make a cup of tea. Cut them out and put them into the correct order. Glue them into your book or on to a piece of paper.

■ Write an instruction under each picture. Use time connectives to show the order. You could use the ones below or choose your own.

next	after that	then	first	finally
when	while	secondly		now
	lastly	until	once	

Illustrations © 2010, Woody Fox.

Assessment

The following grid shows the main objectives and activities covered in this chapter. You can use the grid to locate activities that cover a particular focus that you are keen to monitor.

Objective	Page	Activity title
To extend knowledge of appropriate and powerful adjectives.	**59** **60** **61**	How are you feeling? Film review Football report
To extend the range of verbs used for particular contexts.	**63** **64** **65**	Action verbs Doing things Bossy verbs
To understand that vocabulary choices vary according to purpose and audience.	**67** **68** **69**	Kids' TV Non-fiction reports Instant messaging
To acquire a range of vocabulary for formal and informal occasions.	**67** **68** **69**	Kids' TV Non-fiction reports Instant messaging
To extend the range of conjunctions and time connectives used to link clauses and sentences.	**71** **72** **73**	Mystery story Time connectives for stories How to make a cup of tea

Observation and record keeping

Assessment should track the children's development in both knowledge and skills. The children's areas of strength and targets for development might be recorded in the following areas:
- understanding of the way adjectives and adverbs add precision and variety to writing
- use of a range of appropriate and interesting descriptive words and phrases in different writing tasks
  - understanding of the importance of verbs in writing and the effect of careful selection

- use appropriate and powerful verbs in writing tasks
- knowledge of the imperative form of verbs and their role in instructions
- understanding that more formal speech and writing require more formal vocabulary, but that informal vocabulary is appropriate in certain contexts
- ability to distinguish between formal and informal vocabulary and choose appropriately
- knowledge and use of a widening range of appropriate conjunctions to join simple sentences
- knowledge of words and phrases that indicate time sequences in chronological writing.

Assessment activity

- **What you need**
Photocopiable page 75 'Adjectives, verbs, conjunctions and connectives', thesauruses (optional).
- **What to do**
The activity assesses the children's understanding of the terms *adjective*, *verb*, *conjunction* and *connective*, but these can be explained and exemplified if desired.

Differentiation

- Let less confident learners work orally with an adult scribing. Rephrase questions where necessary. For parts 4 and 5, give appropriate conjunctions and connectives for the children to choose from.
- Challenge more confident children to be adventurous with vocabulary. Ask them to suggest a range of alternatives and explain the effect of each choice. For part 4, let the children experiment with different conjunctions and clause order.

Further learning

- **Distinguishing conjunctions:** Take opportunities, during shared and guided reading and writing, to identify and distinguish between conjunctions and connectives.
- **Role play:** Use role play and provide different audiences and purposes for writing to reinforce formal and informal language choices in different contexts.
- **Audiences:** Encourage the children to read their writing aloud to different audiences to evaluate the effect of descriptive vocabulary choices, including adjectives, adverbs and verbs.

Assessment

Adjectives, verbs, conjunctions and connectives

■ Add an appropriate adjective to each sentence.

I climbed the _____ mountain.

A _____ castle stood on the hilltop.

We dived into the _____ sea.

■ Underline the verb in this sentence.

Mr Jolly walked into the classroom.

■ Write four other verbs you could use instead.

_____   _____   _____   _____

■ Join the two sentences with a conjunction to make one sentence.

I was going to eat the sweets _____ I saved them for my sister.

I can't go swimming _____ I have forgotten my swimming trunks.

I couldn't go out _____ my dad came home.

■ Add a connective to each of these instructions.

How to make a butterfly card

_____ fold a sheet of black paper in half.

_____ draw half a butterfly on one side

of the folded shape and cut it out.

_____ make a card from a different-

coloured piece of card folded in half.

_____ glue the butterfly on to the front

of the card.

Illustrations © 2010, Woody Fox.

Word of the week

The Word of the week pages provide information on one word linked to each section in the chapter. Each word is described in some of the following categories: word definition, word origin, word family, alternative words, fascinating facts and activities. Not all categories are relevant to every word.

You can use the words as a focus to support your work on the different sections of the chapter. For example, you could create a display around it. The information is a starting point for a word focus. The words could form part of your classroom living word bank.

You could also use the word of the week as a springboard to inspire children to think about or research fascinating facts about words, find interesting quotations and to encourage them to use dictionaries and thesauruses.

Electrifying

- **Word definition:** An adjective used in everyday language to mean thrilling or exciting. The word actually, of course, is related to electricity. *To electrify* literally means to charge or provide with electric power.
- **Word origin:** From the new (Renaissance) Latin adjective *electricus* (from classical Latin *electrum*, meaning amber), first used to describe the static electricity properties of amber.
- **Word family:** Verb: *electrify, electrified.*
- **Alternative words:** Breathtaking, exciting, exhilarating, gripping, thrilling.
- **Fascinating facts:** Sir Thomas Browne coined the word *electricity*. An electrick was an object capable of attracting light objects, such as paper, through friction. A piece of amber is an electrick. So *electricity* was the property of behaving like an electrick, in the same way that *elasticity* is the property of behaving like elastic.
- **Activities:** Introduce the word in science and explore the variations: *electric, electricity, electrical, electrically, electrician*. Let the children have fun drawing pictures using the literal meaning, from descriptions such as *a wonderful performance that electrified the audience* and *an electrifying match*.

> **Linked section:**
> Adjectives and adverbs, page 58

March

- **Word definition:** A verb meaning to walk in a military manner or with regular paces.
- **Word origin:** From the Latin *marcus*, meaning a hammer.
- **Word family:** Noun: *march*; verb: *marches, marching, marched.*
- **Alternative words:** Pace, parade, step, stride, strut, troop.
- **Fascinating facts:** A march is a piece of music originally played by a military band. It has a clear two-beat rhythm that an army walked (marched) to. It can be played at any speed and Napoleon Bonaparte adopted a 120 beats (steps) a minute tempo to get his army moving faster. Try it using a metronome.
- **Activities:** Play a range of marches with different tempos, listening first for the two-beat rhythm. Invite the children to use percussion instruments to demonstrate the rhythm and speed and march in formation in the hall or playground, as an army. The *Transit of Venus March* (John Philip Sousa) sets a good pace, and the children will probably be familiar with *The Imperial March* (Darth Vader's theme, John Williams) from the Star Wars films.

> **Linked section:**
> Verbs, page 62

Okay

- **Word definition:** Used colloquially in many languages to show approval or agreement. It also features in computer dialogue boxes. It can be spelled in different ways and is sometimes just *OK*, or even *k* in a text message.
- **Word origin:** Its etymology is disputed, but it may come from the USA in the 1830s when it was fashionable to abbreviate and deliberately misspell words. *OK* may have been an abbreviation for *oll korrekt* (all correct). It was then used as a slogan by an American presidential candidate in 1840, who came from a place known as Old Kinderhook.
- **Alternative words:** All right, fine, right.
- **Fascinating facts:** Okay can be used as a noun (*I need to get your okay for this*), adjective (*the sandwich was okay*), verb (*I need you to okay that*), adverb (*I did okay in the exam*) and on its own.
- **Activities:** Challenge the children to listen for and use the word in as many ways as possible (noun, adjective, verb and adverb). By overusing it, perhaps the children will become aware of the need to vary their vocabulary, while acknowledging, however, that it is a perfectly appropriate word to use colloquially and serves its purpose well.

> **Linked section:**
> Formal and informal language, page 66

Eventually

- **Word definition:** An adverb, meaning finally.
- **Word origin:** From the Latin *eventus*, meaning an occurrence, and from *evenire*, meaning to come out.
- **Word family:** Noun: *event, eventuality, venue*; adjective: *eventful, eventual*.
- **Alternative words:** After a long time, at last, at length, at long last, finally, in due course, in the end, someday, sooner or later, ultimately.
- **Fascinating facts:** *Eventuality* was originally a term from the science of phrenology, where people claimed to be able to discover personality traits from the bumps on people's heads. *Eventuality* was the power of the memory to recall the chronological order of events.
- **Activities:** Encourage the children to use *eventually* as an effective time connective in narrative.

> **Linked section:**
> Conjunctions and connectives, page 70

Fun with words

. . . .

Use these activities to support the vocabulary work in this chapter. They could be used as starter or plenary activities.

Adjectives for nouns
● Prepare a list of suitable nouns. Choose two children to stand up. Call out a noun. The first of the two children to say an appropriate adjective wins. That player stays standing and faces a new challenger. Vary the game by working around the class, alternating nouns and adjectives. For example, give a noun as a starting point, such as *hair*. The next player gives an appropriate adjective, such as *long*. The next person gives a noun that could be long, such as *book*, then another adjective and so on. Players must not repeat words.

Yes or no
● Think of an adjective (or other word class) that children must guess by asking questions that can be answered by *yes* or *no*, such as *Does it describe size?* and *Is it a colour?*

Object
● Pass an interesting object around the circle. Each person must use a different adjective to describe it.

Inventive adjectives
● Before playing, prepare a list of nouns and five (or more) adjectives to describe each. Call out a noun and ask the children to write five appropriate adjectives. Points are awarded for adjectives not on your list.

The teacher's cat
● Invite the children to think up alternative adjectives to describe the teacher's cat. For example, *The teacher's cat is an angry cat, a beautiful cat, a cautious cat…*

PE verbs
● Reinforce verbs in PE, such as *Show me three verbs that happen close to the ground or What verbs can you do on that apparatus?*

Performing actions
● Ask a child to leave the room while the others choose an adverb, such as *quickly*. When the child returns they should ask individuals to perform an action, such as *jump up and down*, in the manner of the chosen adverb. Can they guess the adverb?

And, because and but
● Give a sentence starter, such as *I walked down the road…* Let the children continue the sentence using the conjunctions *and*, *because* and *but*. For example, *I walked down the road **because** I was meeting my friend **but** I tripped over a stone **and** hurt my leg.*

Fill in the gaps
● Prepare sentences from a story. Leave gaps where adjectives, adverbs, verbs and conjunctions could be inserted. In groups, ask the children to suggest appropriate words. Award points for particularly appropriate, original, adventurous and humorous vocabulary.

Chapter 4

Cross-curricular vocabulary

Introduction

In this chapter the children explore vocabulary related to other subjects across the curriculum, specifically geography, history, mathematics and science. All subjects have technical terms for important concepts and the children should learn these as a tool to consolidate implicit understanding. The activities will be used alongside practical engagement with each subject and topic to give contexts for developing the vocabulary.

In this chapter

Geography page 81	To develop a range of vocabulary associated with different types of weather, climate and other natural phenomena.
History page 85	To learn historical vocabulary related to chronology, invasion and settlement, and historical enquiry.
Mathematics page 89	To learn mathematical vocabulary related to data handling, 2D shapes and operations.
Science page 93	To learn vocabulary related to investigations in science, materials and healthy eating topics.
Assessment page 97	Activities and ideas to assess use of mathematical vocabulary related to data handling, 2D shape and operations.

Poster notes

Time (page 80)
The poster provides the opportunity for the children to generate and review the vocabulary of time. Items in the classroom and the view through the window enable discussion of time in a range of curriculum areas and contexts, including mathematics (clocks, timetables), geography (seasons), history (dates, historical periods), and science (night and day, life cycles). Ask the children to suggest all the words on the theme of time that the poster makes them think of. This can be used as a prompt specifically for activities in the Geography (weather and climate) and History (chronology) sections and to make cross-curricular links at other opportunities.

Time

Cross-curricular vocabulary

Geography

Objective

To develop a range of vocabulary associated with different types of weather, climate and other natural phenomena.

Background knowledge

Weather is an integral part of the children's lives, affecting the clothes they wear, which activities they can do and what they see and hear around them. They will be aware of how often adults talk about the weather. They may listen to or watch daily weather reports in various media (or may be encouraged to do so), and note news items about extreme weather and other natural disasters around the world. Use these activities to develop technical vocabulary within a geography topic or when relevant opportunities arise. The children will also develop a descriptive vocabulary that can be used for poetry or story writing.

Activities

The children will generate vocabulary related to different types of weather, fill in and match technical words related to weather and different types of climate, and learn words for disastrous natural phenomena.

- **Photocopiable page 82 'Weather words'**
A collection of newspaper weather forecasts and, if possible, recordings of television forecasts, will ensure that the children have a context and resource for this activity. Share the children's prior knowledge of different types of weather, beginning a bank of descriptive words. Let the children use a range of resources (books, newspapers, websites and thesauruses) to complete the activity. Use the words generated for poetry or as a resource for story writing (for settings, for example).

- **Photocopiable page 83 'Weather and climate'**
Encourage the children to use dictionaries and other relevant resources (geography textbooks and websites) to confirm the meanings of the technical vocabulary. Invite the children to discuss the meanings in pairs. Extend the activity by asking the children to work in groups to research each climate type and extend their vocabulary (*North Pole*, *South Pole*, *equator*, *rainforest*, *continent*).
- **Photocopiable page 84 'Natural disasters'**
This activity works best as a response to a recent event, at home or abroad, using news footage as a stimulus. Put the children in pairs or groups to research and develop word banks for each phenomenon. Develop this into a drama activity, exploring associated sights, sounds and feelings. The word bank (page 125) will provide a starting point.

Further ideas

- **Display:** Use vocabulary generated in activities for displays on the weather, seasons or natural disasters.
- **Weather forecasts:** Compare the more precise, reduced language of weather forecasts with the language used to describe weather in poetry, exploring audience and purpose. The shipping forecast is a fascinating, formulaic version of weather reporting. The patterns and rhythms make it an almost poetic performance, which the children could stage. Use it as a starting point for the children to parody and invent their own versions. See www.answers.com/topic/sea-areas for information and ideas.

 **What's on the CD-ROM**

On the CD-ROM you will find:
- Printable versions of all three photocopiable pages.
- Answers to 'Weather and climate' and 'Natural disasters'.
- Interactive versions of 'Weather words' and 'Natural disasters'.

Name:

Weather words

■ Think of all the words you can to describe these different types of weather. Write them below the shapes.

■ Use other sources to add more words.

_____

_____

_____

_____

_____

_____

_____

_____

_____

_____

_____

_____

Illustrations © 2010, Woody Fox.

Geography

Weather and climate

■ Fill in the gaps of this encyclopedia extract, using the words in the box below.

The conditions of heat, cold, wetness and cloudiness at a particular place and time is known as _____.

_____ is the combination of all the elements of weather at a particular place over long periods of time.

A _____ is a period of the year when the weather tends to have particular features. Meteorologists measure the degree of hotness, called _____, and the amount of moisture that falls from the sky, such as rain, snow or hail, known as _____ and try to predict, or _____, future weather patterns.

| precipitation | temperature | forecast |
| season | weather | climate |

■ Draw a line to match each climate type to its description.

polar		hot and wet all year
cool temperate		hot and dry all year
warm temperate		very cold all year
desert		cold winters, warm summers, rain all year
tropical		mild wet winters, hot dry summers

Name:

Natural disasters

■ Natural disasters are changes that are so great they may damage the shape of the land or the lives of people and other living things.

■ Great changes happen deep inside the Earth and on its surface. The changes on the outer part of the Earth happen because of different types of weather. Match each word to its description.

volcano	a whirling windstorm with a long, funnel-shaped cloud reaching to the ground
hurricane	a violent shaking of the ground
avalanche	an overflow of water, from a river or the sea
tornado	a river of rock, earth and other debris saturated with water
drought	a sudden movement of snow, ice and rock down a mountainside
flood	a very strong windstorm
landslide	the erupting of gases and hot lava from an opening in the Earth's crust
earthquake	a mass of rock, earth and debris moving down a slope
mudflow	a lack of rain for a long time

History

Objective

To learn historical vocabulary related to chronology, invasion and settlement, and historical enquiry.

Background knowledge

Children often find it difficult to understand the concept of time and chronology and how long ago events occurred. Time vocabulary can be complex because we have different ways and conventions for describing time. As well as notions of time encountered in mathematics (*minutes*, *hours*, *days*, *months*, *dates*), there are vague phrases (*long ago*, *in ancient times*), words that describe time spans (*generation*, *reign*, *decade*), terms for large but inexact amounts of time (*age*, *period*) and for smaller but exact amounts of time (*Victorian*, *the Fifties*).

Activities

The children learn words related to chronology through a matching activity, sort words into 'invasion' and 'settlement' categories and fill in words in a text about historical enquiry.

● **Photocopiable page 86 'Vocabulary of time'**
The activity could be used in different ways, beginning either with the words or with the definitions. Less confident learners may need to work with more specific time words, for example, to order *minute*, *hour* and *day*, or to develop their understanding of *before*, *after* and *later*. *Age*, *era* and *generation* may prove valuable starting points for further discussion, exploring everyday meanings alongside specifically historical ones. Encourage the children to compile a class glossary, adding new words and drawing on the word bank (page 125).

● **Photocopiable page 87 'Invasion and settlement'**
Use this activity as an introduction to a specific topic, such as the Romans, Anglo-Saxons, Vikings, Normans, the Second World War or 20th century movement and settlement. Encourage the children to use dictionaries to check meanings of unknown words and discuss and justify their decisions. Use this activity as the basis for drama and writing in role.

● **Photocopiable page 88 'How do we find out about the past?'**
Do this activity as part of practical work on historical skills. Provide dictionaries and appropriate textbooks where necessary. Some children will need support to read, rephrase and interpret the text. Reinforce the vocabulary by exploring meanings and word origins, such as *primary*, *secondary*, *source*, *artefact*, *excavate* and *archaeologist*.

Further ideas

● **Number words:** Use maths skills to explore number words 'dec-', 'cent-' and 'mill-'. Note the origin of the word *chronology* itself (the Greek *chronos*, meaning time, and *logia*, meaning study) and other words beginning with 'chron-' or ending with '-logy'.
● **Language in context:** Use examples from news items, for example, to discuss and reinforce the vocabulary of time and of invasion and settlement.
● **Fact and opinion:** Reinforce these historical words and concepts by providing statements, related to any topic, and ask the children to distinguish fact from opinion. Ask them to make up their own facts and opinions about a favourite sport, team or pop group, for example, for others to differentiate.

 **What's on the CD-ROM**

On the CD-ROM you will find:
● Printable versions of all three photocopiable pages.
● Answers to all three photocopiable pages.
● Interactive versions of all three photocopiable pages.

History

Vocabulary of time

■ Work with a partner or a small group. Cut out both sets of cards and keep the two sets separate. Spread each set out on the table and try to match each word with its definition.

age or era	reign	chronology	decade
century	millennium	generation	AD (Anno Domini)
BC (Before Christ)	past	present	future

A period of 1000 years.	The portion of time that is happening now.	The portion of time that has not yet happened.	'In the year of the Lord.' Used to number the years since the birth of Christ.
A period of ten years.	The time during which a person or thing has lived or existed.	Used to number the years before the birth of Christ.	A period of 100 years.
All the people living at the same time or of approximately the same age.	The order of events in time.	The time during which a king or queen rules.	The portion of time that has already happened.

History

Invasion and settlement

■ Work with a partner or in a small group. Cut out the cards and spread them on the table. Put **invasion** and **settlement** at the top of the table.

■ Discuss and decide which heading you think each word belongs to. Use a dictionary if you need to.

invasion	settlement
emigration	immigration
refugee	empire
power	occupation
community	attack
cooperate	oppose
subdue	raid
conquest	trade
hostile	rule
welcome	authority
visit	colony
enemy	resident
peace	stay
dominate	migrant

Name:

History

How do we find out about the past?

■ Choose the correct word from this box to fill each gap in the text.

primary sources	evidence	archaeologists	investigate
sources	interpret	accounts	fact	excavate
interview	opinion	artefacts	secondary sources

We use different types of _____ to _____ people's

lives and events in the past and how things have changed.

We can look at different _____ of information, such as

photographs, paintings, books, letters, buildings, maps, plans and objects.

_____ give us first-hand information. They are _____

such as letters, photographs, articles of clothing and other items that have survived

from the past. We can also _____ people who were there at the

time. Many objects from the past are found by _____, who dig up,

or _____, historical sites.

_____ give us second-hand information. They are

_____ of the past created by people writing or drawing about

events some time after they happened. A historian has to _____

this evidence to decide whether it is _____ (something that actually

happened) or _____ (what someone thinks about what happened).

Illustrations © 2010, Woody Fox.

Mathematics

Objective

To learn mathematical vocabulary related to data handling, 2D shapes and operations.

Background knowledge

As in all subjects, children need to learn to use appropriate vocabulary in mathematics. Correct terminology is essential for real understanding of concepts, but it needs to be built up gradually and revisited regularly, in context and with plenty of practical examples. Some words have an everyday sense as well as a specific mathematical meaning, such as *frequency*, *pattern* and *difference*, so the children need to develop this specific understanding. The children need to be able to think flexibly about operations and carry out calculations in different ways. The vocabulary emphasises these different approaches.

Activities

The children match data handling vocabulary to definitions, describe and label 2D shapes, and group words according to the operations they describe.

● **Photocopiable page 90 'Data handling vocabulary'**
Let the children complete this activity over time, as they cover different aspects of data handling, or use it as a review or revision of vocabulary. Model use of the language in context and encourage the children to describe processes, orally and in writing, using appropriate vocabulary. Make further cross-curricular links to investigations in science.

● **Photocopiable page 91 '2D shapes'**
Ensure that the children are aware of regular and irregular polygons. Explore roots of word parts, such as 'tri-' (three), 'quad-' (four), 'pent-' (five) and '-lateral'

(side). Extend this to explore the names for other shapes, such as *equilateral* (Latin for equal sides) and *isosceles* (Greek for equal legs) *triangles*. Invite the children to write descriptions for others to guess the shape. For example, *I have five sides, all the same size, and five equal angles. What am I?*

● **Photocopiable page 92 'Operations'**
Support an understanding of the vocabulary using practical examples. Encourage the children to make a display of words and examples. For example, *difference* could be illustrated with two towers of bricks of different heights. Ask the children to write sums using words instead of symbols for each other, using the correct vocabulary.

Further ideas

● **Other polygons:** Investigate other numerical prefixes. For example, ask the children to predict what a polygon with seven or nine sides would be called.
● **Feely bags:** Provide shapes in feely bags. Let the children take turns to feel a shape in the bag and describe it, using appropriate vocabulary, for others to name or draw.
● **Data-handling challenges:** Invite the children to work in groups to devise data collection, representation and interpretation challenges and to write instructions for other groups to follow.
● **Shape poetry:** Write shape poetry. Choose a 2D shape and list as many words as you can to describe it or objects of that shape, such as *circle – round*, *curved*, *rolling*, *sun*, *pizza* and *wheel*. Write triangular, circular or square-shaped poems.

What's on the CD-ROM

On the CD-ROM you will find:
● Printable versions of all three photocopiable pages.
● Answers to all three photocopiable pages.
● Interactive versions of 'Data handling vocabulary' and 'Operations'.

Name:

Mathematics

Data handling vocabulary

■ These are words used to talk about data handling. Choose the correct word to match each definition and write it in the box. The first one has been done for you.

frequency	pattern	represent	estimate	criterion
classify	interpret	compare	data	tally
survey	relationship	measure	predict	

A set of facts or information.	data
How often something occurs.	
To count items and make a mark for each.	
To suggest what may happen, based on known information.	
A regular or repeated arrangement or sequence of items.	
A connection or association between pieces of information.	
The collection of information from a group of people.	
To note similarities and differences between things.	
To arrange things into groups with similar features.	
To display information in a particular way.	
To read and understand information.	
To make a sensible guess about an amount or a size.	
To find the amount or size of something using suitable equipment.	
A specific feature that you use to sort information into groups.	

Mathematics

2D shapes

■ Write a description of each shape using these words. The first one has been done for you.

sides   curved   straight   angles   right angle   equal

■ Label each shape with its name.

circle	triangle	quadrilateral
pentagon	rectangle	hexagon
square	octagon	right-angled triangle

three straight sides and three angles triangle		

Name:

Mathematics

Operations

■ These words can all be used to describe the operations in the boxes. Write each word into the correct box. The first one has been done for you.

~~add~~	multiplied by	share equally	subtract	product
more than	multiplication	take away	total	
subtraction	division	plus	times	divided into
minus	sum	less than	share	difference
divide	multiply	divided by	addition	

add **+**	**–**
÷	**X**

Science

Objective

To learn vocabulary related to investigations in science, materials and healthy eating topics.

Background knowledge

Children need to move from using everyday language to increasingly precise use of technical and scientific vocabulary. Words used to describe materials may have everyday senses, but the children need to learn their scientific uses as describers of properties, which in turn allows the children to consider uses of materials. The children's understanding of what constitutes a balanced and healthy diet will be supported by a knowledge of the ways in which different types of food contribute to efficient functioning of the body, using appropriate terminology. Practical activities will enable the children to use language in context and they will gradually take responsibility for planning their own systematic investigations.

Activities

Children will match properties of materials to their scientific definitions, choose correct words to complete a text about healthy eating and select vocabulary to describe different stages of an investigation.

● **Photocopiable page 94 'Properties of materials'**
Encourage the children to work in pairs or small groups to discuss the materials and their properties. Ask them to provide examples of materials with the given properties, finding classroom items or drawing pictures. Use the words and descriptions as labels for an interactive display, for class or individual glossaries, or as a starting point for a class non-fiction book about materials.

● **Photocopiable page 95 'Healthy eating'**
The vocabulary here is quite challenging. Provide dictionaries and appropriate reference texts for the children to check the meanings of the words. Encourage plenty of discussion about the scientific vocabulary to consolidate the children's understanding. Invite them to make information leaflets on healthy eating to distribute around the school.

● **Photocopiable page 96 'Investigations'**
The children will learn the technical vocabulary of systematic enquiry alongside questions in everyday language to reinforce understanding. Show the children how to make their own planning frameworks using the suggested headings. These can be laminated for reuse in the future. Introduce other words, such as *method*, *outcome*, *data*, *interpret*, *explanation* and *conclusion*.

Further ideas

● **Synonyms:** As a literacy extension, ask the children to use thesauruses to find synonyms for the words in the materials activity, reinforcing their understanding of the concepts while emphasising the correct, scientific vocabulary. Let them also explore metaphorical uses of the vocabulary, such as a *rigid attitude* (unwilling to change an opinion) or a *transparent lie* (easily found out), linking them to scientific meanings.

● **Science calligrams:** Encourage the children to illustrate meanings of words such as *flexible*, *magnetic* and *waterproof* as calligrams.

● **Packaging:** Collect food packaging for display. Using the vocabulary learned, invite the children to label and describe the nutritional content of different items.

 **What's on the CD-ROM**

On the CD-ROM you will find:
● Printable versions of all three photocopiable pages.
● Answers to all three photocopiable pages.
● Interactive versions of 'Properties of materials' and 'Investigations'.

Name:

Science

Properties of materials

■ Below are words that are used to describe the properties of materials. Cut out the cards and match each property to its definition.

natural	flexible	transparent
elastic	translucent	absorbent
magnetic	waterproof	opaque
brittle	rigid	manufactured
not made by humans	easily broken	attracted to a magnet
made by humans, by hand or using tools or machines	able to stretch and return to its original shape	allows light to pass through
easily bent	able to soak up liquid	allows some light to pass through
not easily bent	not allowing liquid to pass through and not able to soak up liquid	allows no light to pass through

■SCHOLASTIC
www.scholastic.co.uk

Science

Healthy eating

■ Choose the right word from the bottom of the page to fit in each gap.

There are five main groups of food.

Bread, cereals and potatoes

This group includes bread, breakfast cereals, pasta and rice. They provide

_____, which give us _____. You should eat at least six

portions a day.

Meat, fish and beans

This group includes meat, chicken, eggs, beans and lentils. They contain

_____, which helps _____ and _____ our

bodies. You should eat two or three portions a day.

Fruit and vegetables

This group includes all fresh, frozen, dried and canned fruit and vegetables,

and juices. They contain _____ and _____, which are

needed to keep every part of the body _____, and _____

which helps our bodies _____ food. You should eat at least five

portions a day.

Dairy

This group includes milk, cheese, cream and yogurt. They contain

_____, which makes strong _____ and _____.

You should eat three or four portions a day.

Fatty and sugary foods

This group includes butter, margarine, cooking oils, biscuits, sweets and fizzy

drinks. _____ and _____ give us a quick _____

of energy, but eating a lot of these foods will make you put on too much

weight and rot your teeth. You should eat them only occasionally.

minerals	vitamins	burst	build	teeth
calcium	protein	bones	fibre	digest
repair	fats	healthy		sugars
	energy		carbohydrates	

Name:

Science

Investigations

■ Choose the right heading for each part of this investigation into magnetic forces. The first one has been done for you.

Our science investigation

_____Question_____ (What do we want to find out?)
Which magnet is the strongest?

_____ (What do you think will happen?)
I think the horseshoe magnet will be the strongest because it is the biggest.

_____ (What will you use?)
Three different magnets, a paperclip, a flat table, a ruler.

_____ (What will you change?)
The magnets.

_____ (What will you keep the same?)
The paperclip, the ruler and the table.

_____ (What will you look at or count?)
I will measure on the ruler the distance that the paperclip moves.

_____ (How will you make a note of what happened?)
I will write the distances on a chart.

Question	Variables	Record	Prediction
Fair test	Measure	Equipment	

Assessment

The following grid shows the main objectives and activities covered in this chapter. You can use the grid to locate activities that cover a particular focus that you are keen to monitor.

Objective	Page	Activity title
To develop a range of vocabulary associated with different types of weather, climate and other natural phenomena.	82 83 84	Weather words Weather and climate Natural disasters
To learn historical vocabulary related to chronology, invasion and settlement, and historical enquiry.	86 87 88	Vocabulary of time Invasion and settlement How do we find out about the past?
To learn mathematical vocabulary related to data handling, 2D shapes and operations.	90 91 92	Data handling vocabulary 2D shapes Operations
To learn vocabulary related to investigations in science, materials and healthy eating topics.	94 95 96	Properties of materials Healthy eating Investigations

Observation and record keeping

Assessment should track the children's development in both knowledge and skills. The children's areas of strength and targets for development might be recorded in the following areas:

- awareness that words may have both everyday and specialised meanings
- understanding that different curriculum subjects, and topics within these, have 'fields' of vocabulary
- developing interest in words and meanings generally, and technical vocabulary specifically
- knowledge of, and ability to use appropriately and in context, a range of subject-specific vocabulary related to particular curriculum areas.

Assessment activity

- **What you need**
Photocopiable page 98 'Words and symbols', dictionaries (optional).
- **What to do**
Although the context here is mathematical, the focus is on words and meanings. You could, of course, ask the children to find the answers to the calculations if appropriate.

Differentiation

- Support less confident learners with reading and let them work with adult support.
- Ask more confident learners to write further word calculations, using this and other vocabulary. Extend the activity to the vocabulary of multiplication and division.

Further learning

- **Technical vocabulary:** Ensure that the children use technical vocabulary at every opportunity, in context and alongside everyday explanations where appropriate, to enable them to build up their understanding gradually.
- **Glossaries:** Encourage the children to build their own glossaries for each subject area and topic, with explanations and examples.

Name:

Words and symbols

■ Rewrite these word calculations using the correct symbol. The first one has been done for you.

14 add 9 _____ $14 + 9$ _____

27 plus 16 _____

56 take away 15 _____

What is the sum of 38 and 23? _____

Find the difference between 45 and 13 _____

Subtract 21 from 65 _____

Increase 24 by 12 _____

What is 15, 8 and 2 altogether? _____

Decrease 25 by 10 _____

76 minus 20 _____

Data handling

■ Read these sentences describing how the children carried out an investigation into favourite colours. Choose the correct word, from the list at the bottom, to fill each gap.

First we _____ which colour we thought would be most

popular. Then we did a _____ by asking each person

which was their favourite colour. We _____ their answers

using a _____ chart. We added up the tallies to find the

_____ of each answer. Then we _____ the

_____ in a bar graph. We wrote questions to find out if our

friends could _____ the graph.

frequency	interpret	data	recorded	predicted
	represented		survey	tally	

Word of the week

The Word of the week pages provide information on one word linked to each section in the chapter. Each word is described in some of the following categories: word definition, word origin, word family, alternative words, fascinating facts and activities. Not all categories are relevant to every word.

You can use the words as a focus to support your work on the different sections of the chapter. For example, you could create a display around it. The information is a starting point for a word focus. The words could form part of your classroom living word bank.

You could also use the word of the week as a springboard to inspire children to think about or research fascinating facts about words, find interesting quotations and to encourage them to use dictionaries and thesauruses.

Spring

- **Word definition:** A noun meaning: a season, a natural source of water, a coil with elastic properties and a leap or bounce. A verb meaning to move suddenly or leap.
- **Word origin:** From the Old English *springan*, from the German *springen*, meaning to leap, burst forth or fly up.
- **Word family:** Adjective: *sprung;* verb: (past tense) *sprang*, (past participle) *sprung*.
- **Alternative words:** Source of water: beginning, fount, fountain, origin, source, well; verb: bounce, bound, hop, jump, leap, pounce, skip, vault.
- **Fascinating facts:** The elastic coil *spring*, named in 1428, originally used in clocks and watches. The word was later used to name the suspension device in carriages and cars. In the 14th century the noun *spring* meant a time of rising or suddenly coming into existence (such as, sunrise, the waxing moon and the rising tide): hence also *spring* the name for the season of new life and growth. The breed of dog, Springer Spaniel, is so named because it *springs* game for hunters to shoot.
- **Activities:** Consider how the different meanings are connected, for example through curriculum areas: seasons and rivers (geography) and forces (science).

Linked section:
Geography, page 81

Refugee

- **Word definition:** A noun meaning a person who flees to another country for refuge (or safety), usually to escape war or religious or political persecution.
- **Word origin:** From the Latin *refugium*, from *fugere*, meaning to flee.
- **Word family:** Noun: *refuge*.
- **Alternative words:** Asylum seeker, displaced person, emigrant, émigré, evacuee, exile, expatriate, fugitive, outcast.
- **Fascinating facts:** World Refugee Day (20 June) aims to raise awareness of refugees' difficulties and need for protection from persecution and economic support.
- **Activities:** Citizenship: encourage the children to explore ideas related to diversity equally, prejudice and persecution. Find synonyms for *refuge* and draw and write about personal safe places. Explore meaning of and connections between words such as *identify*, *diversity*, *respect*, *tolerance*, *fairness*, *rights* and *responsibilities*. The class or school could be the context, but news items may encourage discussion in a global context. Investigate other words with the suffix '-ee' such as *trainee*, *evacuee*, *interviewee*, *absentee* and *escapee*, to work out what the suffix means.

Linked section:
History, page 85

Right (angle)

- **Word definition:** An adjective with multiple meanings, most commonly meaning the opposite of left, and correct or true.
- **Word origin:** There may be two different roots, one meaning the opposite of left (from the German *recht)* and the other, true or straight (from the Latin *rectus*). These may be connected, because the right hand was considered to be the correct hand in many contexts.

Linked section:
Mathematics,
page 89

- **Word family:** Adjective: *rightful, rightfully*; adverb: *rightly.*
- **Alternative words:** Accurate, correct, exact, fair, genuine, good, honest, just, lawful, moral, proper, straight, suitable, true, valid.
- **Fascinating facts:** The Latin word *dexter* also meant right, giving rise to *dexterity* and *dextrous*, with their positive connotations of clever with the hands. Latin for left was *sinister*, with its connotations today of something evil, ominous or unlucky. Right-handedness was correct and desirable, left-handedness was incorrect and undesirable. Until recently, children were made to use right hands from an early age.
- **Activities:** Using dictionaries and thesauruses, investigate the meaning *right*. Connect the various meanings and work out why a right angle is so called. Mathematics: explore shapes with right angles and vocabulary for other types of angle (straight, acute, obtuse). Can they make connections between the various meanings and work out why a right angle is so called? As a mathematics task, explore shapes with right angles and vocabulary for other types of angle (straight, acute, obtuse). Citizenship: explore right and wrong, and rights and responsibilities. Literacy: make a word web for *right*, using synonyms for different shades of meaning. Explore expressions with the word *right*, such as *all right, right as rain, right-hand man, in one's right mind* and *right on.*

Natural

Linked section:
Science, page 93

- **Word definition:** An adjective meaning relating to, produced by or according to nature, not the work of humans.
- **Word origin:** From the Latin *naturalis*, meaning by birth or according to nature (from the Latin *natura*, meaning innate characteristics or qualities or the normal course of things).
- **Word family:** Noun: *nature, naturalist*; adverb: *naturally*; verb: *naturalise.*
- **Alternative words:** Common, everyday, genuine, hereditary, inborn, inherited, innate, instinctive, intuitive, native, normal, not artificial, sincere, standard, typical, unpretentious, unprocessed, unrefined, untaught, usual.
- **Fascinating facts:** *Nature* is often used to mean the outdoor world and particularly animals and plants, as in *I love nature*. The Natural History Museum defines nature as botany (all forms of plant life), entomology (insects), mineralogy (rocks, soils and minerals), palaeontology (fossils) and zoology (all forms of animal life).
- **Activities:** On the Natural History Museum website (www.nhm.ac.uk) find out what is included in the term *natural*. Learn words for classifying the natural world. Help the children distinguish natural from human-made materials. Contrast with *manufactured*, originally meaning made by hand (from the Latin *manu*, meaning hand, and *factura*, meaning working), now meaning made by machinery. *Manufactured* also means *fabricated, concocted* or *invented* (with negative connotations).

Fun with words

· ·

Use these activities to support the vocabulary work in this chapter. They could be used as starter or plenary activities.

Definitions
● Make sets of cards for relevant themes, with a word on one side and its definition on the other. Challenge the children to work out the word from the definition or vice versa. These could be made into 'loop' cards – one child reads the definition on their card and another child has the word described, then reads the definition from their card and so on.

Acrostic poems
● Tell the children to write acrostic poems, using a word from a relevant topic as a starting point, such as *thunder*, *transparent* or *multiplication*.

Topic
● Ask the children to write down as many words as they can, in a given time, related to a particular topic. Award points for the individual, pair or group with the most correctly spelled words. Try this before, during and after working on a topic. Extend this by asking the children to group their words into verbs, nouns and adjectives.

Topic alphabet
● Ask the children to find a topic word beginning with each letter of the alphabet, such as *avalanche*, *blizzard*, *cloud*, *drizzle* and so on. It will be difficult for some letters, so this could be a long-term challenge.

Weather mime
● Let the children mime different weather conditions for others to guess.

Shape picture
● Ask the children to draw pictures using shapes from your instructions, such as a square house, with a right-angled triangle for a roof and two rectangular windows.

Odd one out
● Provide groups of words related to a particular topic with an odd one out for the children to find, such as *circle*, *triangle*, *hexagon*, *sphere* and *square* (where *sphere* is a 3D shape in a group of 2D shapes); or *minus*, *subtract*, *difference*, *plus* and *decrease* (where *plus* is for addition in a group of subtraction words).

Silly questions
● In science, ask silly questions, such as *Why couldn't you use a plastic towel?* or *Why couldn't a raincoat be made of paper?* The children will know that these are silly, but need to explain why.

Bingo
● Play Bingo with topic words, where the children write down five relevant words. The first to tick off all their words, as you call them out, is the winner. Alternatively write topic words on cards and distribute to the children. Call out a letter. If that letter is in the word on a player's card, they take one step forward, or two steps if it appears twice.

Chapter 5

Fun with words

Introduction

This chapter looks at words and their meanings in a range of different ways, encouraging the children's curiosity and interest. They will learn ways in which signs and symbols sometimes replace words to communicate and how words themselves can be combined and linked to create new meanings and layers of meaning. The children can have fun exploring common phrases and expressions and then create original ideas of their own.

Poster notes

Animal similes (page 103)
The poster gives examples of animal similes, using both *as* and *like*. It can be used as an introduction to photocopiable page 115 'Animal similes'. Ask the children to name the illustrated animals and discuss why each animal is associated with a particular characteristic. Some are quite literal comparisons, such as *run like a deer*, but others are more metaphorical, as in *proud as a peacock*, and so will generate more discussion.

In this chapter

Signs and symbols page 104	To learn that signs and symbols sometimes replace words to represent and communicate ideas and meanings. To learn to 'read' a range of common signs and symbols.
New words page 108	To learn that portmanteau words are invented by blending parts of two words to make a new word that combines the sense of both.
Collocations and similes page 112	To learn how words are commonly linked together in collocations and similes.
Playing with meaning page 116	To learn that the sounds of some words imitate their meanings.
Assessment page 120	To assess knowledge of common collocations and similes.

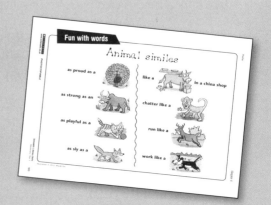

Fun with words

Animal similes

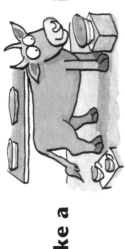

like a _____ in a china shop

chatter like a

run like a

work like a

as proud as a

as strong as an

as playful as a

as sly as a

Illustrations © 2010, Woody Fox.

Signs and symbols

Objectives

To learn that signs and symbols sometimes replace words to represent and communicate ideas and meanings. To learn to 'read' a range of common signs and symbols.

Background knowledge

Signs often give directions or instructions, whereas symbols are usually pictures or shapes that have a particular meaning. They are used to save time, by being instantly recognisable, communicating without words, and can be understood by people who speak different languages. A washing care symbol is a pictogram. These symbols are more-or-less universal and often correspond to programmes on automatic washing machines. Brown and white tourism road signs help visitors find places of interest easily. They may also use words, such as the name of the site. Semaphore conveys information across long distances using two flags, one in each hand. Each letter of the alphabet is represented by a different position of the flags. Developed for use at sea in the 19th century, sometimes it is still used on ships, using burning torches at night.

Activities

These activities help the children to understand the purpose and work out the meanings of symbols, signs and semaphore.

● **Photocopiable page 105 'Washing care symbols'**
Ask the children to look at the washing labels on their clothes. Explain that for washing, the symbol for the temperature needs to be combined with the type of wash suggested. To extend, invite the children to make up their own washing labels for others to read.

● **Photocopiable page 106 'Tourism signs'**
Show the children pictures of brown and white tourism signs and share the background information above. Ask the children to discuss with a partner what they think the signs represent, before giving out the photocopiable sheet. Let the children look up any words in dictionaries if necessary. Encourage the children to design their own signs for tourist attractions or places in your local area.

● **Photocopiable page 107 'Semaphore'**
Demonstrate some semaphore signs so the children understand how they work. Note that the image is seen from the 'reader's' perspective. Take the children to a large space and let them spell out words or messages to each other. Try using words related to a current curriculum topic.

Further ideas

● **Symbols across the curriculum:** Make a display of symbols used in each curriculum area, such as punctuation in English, operations in mathematics and map symbols in geography.
● **Signs and symbols everywhere:** Find signs around the school or local area and consider their purpose, content and design. Design and make signs for the school office, staffroom or hall, and instructions for the classroom, such as *No talking*. Explore other signs and symbols, such as traffic signs, religious symbols and school badges.
● **Other alphabets:** Explore ways of representing the alphabet, such as Morse code, the NATO phonetic alphabet, Braille and the British Sign Language Fingerspelling alphabet.

What's on the CD-ROM

On the CD-ROM you will find:
● Printable versions of all three photocopiable pages.
● Answers to all three photocopiable pages.
● Interactive versions of 'Tourism signs' and 'Semaphore'.

Signs and symbols

Washing care symbols

■ All clothes have a label with symbols that tell you how they should be washed, dried and ironed.

Washing	
Machine wash at 95° or less	95
Machine wash at 60° or less	60
Machine wash at 50° or less	50
Machine wash at 40° or less	40
Machine wash at 30° or less	30
Cotton wash	
Synthetic wash	
Wool wash	
Hand wash only	
Do not wash	

Drying	
Dry flat	
Hang dry	
Drip dry	
May be tumble dried	
Tumble dry at low setting	
Tumble dry at high setting	
Do not tumble dry	

Bleaching	
Chlorine bleach allowed in cold and diluted solution	CL
Do not use chlorine bleach	

Ironing	
Iron at maximum temperature of 110°	
Iron at maximum temperature of 150°	
Iron at maximum temperature of 200°	
Do not iron	

■ Read these labels and write down how each garment should be cared for.

Name:

Tourism signs

■ These are signs that you might see at the side of the road. They show the location of places of interest that tourists might want to visit. The signs are usually brown with white symbols.

■ Choose the right label from the box below for each sign.

nature reserve   building of historic interest   youth hostel
theatre   picnic area   pleasure or theme park   campsite
museum   battlefield site

PHOTOCOPIABLE   **■SCHOLASTIC**
www.scholastic.co.uk

Signs and symbols

Semaphore

■ Semaphore is a way of sending messages across long distances using two flags, one in each hand. Each letter of the alphabet is represented by a different position of the flags.

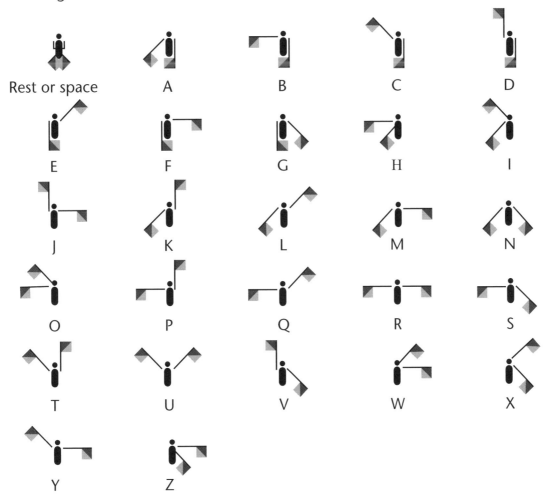

■ Can you read this message and answer the question?

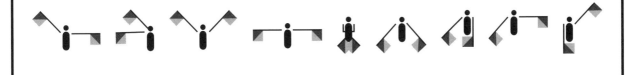

_____

New words

Objective

To learn that portmanteau words are invented by blending parts of two words to make a new word that combines the sense of both.

Background knowledge

The word *portmanteau* (a large travelling bag, from the French *porte*, meaning carry, and *manteau*, meaning coat) suggests more than one meaning packed into a word. Lewis Carroll coined the term in *Alice Through the Looking Glass*, where Humpty Dumpty invents words, such as *slithy* (*slimy* and *lithe*). The endings '-thon' and '-holic' are not genuine suffixes but corruptions or extensions of the original meaning. '-athon' (from *marathon*) is usually linked to fund-raising activities. Words ending with '-olic' or '-aholic' mean doing something to excess or not being able to stop doing something. They can be interpreted as 'addicted to' (from the original *alcoholic*), but they can also mean someone who really enjoys something.

Activities

The activities explore common portmanteau words and encourage the children to invent portmanteau animal names.

● **Photocopiable page 109 'Common portmanteau words'**
Read the text extract with the children and share prior knowledge. Discuss the meaning of *portmanteau*. Evaluate the children's own portmanteau words, discussing spelling and pronunciation. Let the children write definitions of the words on the photocopiable sheet for a portmanteau dictionary.

● **Photocopiable page 110 'Inventing words'**
Encourage the children to make the 'long-distance' link between *marathon* and the new words. Be sensitive if the word *alcoholic* comes up. Let the children have fun making up and defining their own words with the same endings, such as *sleepathon* and *tellyholic*, and using them in dialogues.

● **Photocopiable page 111 'Strange animals'**
Some children may need support to combine words (or parts) into a pronounceable whole. Ask the children to describe to their partner or group what their animal would look like. As a follow-up activity, tell the children to draw their new animals.

Further ideas

● **More portmanteaux:** A number of websites give lists of portmanteau words for the children to explore. Let the children also invent more portmanteau words of their own. For example, *overflow* and *explode* gives *oversplode*, which is what porridge does in the microwave if you leave it too long. More simply, show them how to combine two nouns commonly found together, such as *food* and *drink* to make *frink*, or words related to a theme, such as fruits (*bananerine*, a cross between *banana* and *tangerine*).

● **Other inventions:** Explore other invented words, such as *fanzine* (from *magazine*) or *burglar-proof* (from *waterproof*).

● **Fundraising:** Ask the children to suggest and organise a range of fundraising '-athon' activities.

● **Advertising:** As in a recent mobile phone advert, *It's so cheap you can afford to be a talkaholic*, invite the children to make up adverts for other '-holics', such as *chocoholic* and *bookaholic*.

 **What's on the CD-ROM**

On the CD-ROM you will find:
● Printable versions of all three photocopiable pages.
● Answers to 'Common portmanteau words' and 'Inventing words'.

New words

Common portmanteau words

Portmanteau word

A portmanteau word is formed by blending parts of two or more words to make a new word, with the combined meanings of both. For example, a **spork** is a cross between a **spoon** and a **fork**. It has a spoon-like shallow scoop with the addition of fork-like prongs so you can both scoop and spear, useful when eating stew, for example. **Brunch** is a combination of **breakfast** and **lunch**. It usually means a meal eaten late in the morning and would include typical breakfast foods, such as eggs and bacon, so you might call it breakfast eaten at lunch time.

■　Look closely at these words and their meanings. Write down the two words that have been combined to form a new word.

Chunnel – a tunnel under the English Channel

Chunnel　=　_____ + _____

intercom – an internal telephone system for communication within a building

intercom　=　_____ + _____

fortnight – a period of two weeks, or fourteen days and nights

fortnight　=　_____ + _____

■　Make portmanteau words from these pairs.

prim + sissy = _____　　　　**squirm + wiggle** = _____

tiger + lion = _____　　　　**banana + toffee** = _____

■　Which two words have been combined to form these portmanteau words? Write definitions for the portmanteau words. Use a dictionary if you need to.

emoticon　= _____ + _____ = _____

ginormous　= _____ + _____ = _____

Eurovision　= _____ + _____ = _____

skyjack　= _____ + _____ = _____

Illustrations © 2010, Woody Fox.

Name:

New words

Inventing words

■ Read this explanation for the origin of the word **marathon**.

What is the origin of the marathon?
There are several versions of the story of how the marathon began. This is one of them.

In 490 BC, the Greeks had defeated the Persian army at Marathon, a town about 26 miles (42 kilometres) from the city of Athens. A messenger called Pheidippides was sent to bring the good news to Athens. He ran the whole distance and just had the strength to pass on his message before he died from heatstroke.

The legend inspired the modern Olympic marathon race, first run in 1896, which is approximately 26 miles and takes just over two hours for athletes to complete. The word **marathon** is sometimes used to mean any event or activity of great time or distance or that needs great stamina or endurance.

People sometimes make up words from words that already exist. The word **marathon**, for a long-distance race, has been used for over 100 years, but more recently new words have been invented from it.

■ What do you think these words mean?

walkathon _____

readathon _____

telethon _____

■ Words ending in **-holic** mean someone who really enjoys doing something or does something all the time. What do you think these words mean?

shopaholic _____

workaholic _____

chocoholic _____

Illustrations © 2010, Woody Fox.

PHOTOCOPIABLE   ■SCHOLASTIC
www.scholastic.co.uk

New words

Strange animals

■ Play with a partner or a small group. Cut out the cards and place them face down in a pile. Take turns to turn over two cards. Try to use both names to make a new animal that is a bit of both of them.

■ In your book or on a sheet of paper, write the names of the animals your pair or group made.

squirrel	fox	bat
hare	weasel	badger
shrew	polecat	vole
rabbit	stoat	deer
seal	dormouse	wildcat
hedgehog	mink	otter

Illustrations © 2010, Woody Fox.

Collocations and similes

Objective

To learn how words are commonly linked together in collocations and similes.

Background knowledge

Collocations are groups of words that are commonly found together, such as *crystal clear*. Colours occur in many collocations, forming idiomatic expressions. A particular form of collocation is a pair of words, usually joined by *and*, such as *loud and clear*. These are called *binomials* (or Siamese twins) and *irreversible binomials* if they do not work in the reverse order. A simile, where one thing is directly compared with another using *as* or *like*, such as *stubborn as a mule*, is a form of collocation because the comparison is predictable. While collocations can be fun, the children should be encouraged to use original phrases and comparisons in their writing.

Activities

The activities encourage the children to recognise common English word pairs and associations between words and ideas.

● **Photocopiable page 113 'Colour collocations'**
Discuss the meaning of *red-handed* (noting the hyphen) and ask the children to use the phrase in a sentence. The children may suggest *house* or *grocer* as collocations for *green*, which can lead to discussion of words as opposed to phrases. Extend the activity by exploring ideas associated with different colours, such as red: *heat*, *anger*, *blood* and *danger*, and inventing original phrases.

● **Photocopiable page 114 'Inseparable pairs'**
Display the poem with the second part of each phrase covered and ask the children to predict the words,

discussing alternatives suggested. Discuss the irreversible nature of the pairs. Ask the children to suggest and research other similar phrases to put into sentences and role plays.

● **Photocopiable page 115 'Animal similes'**
Use poster page 103 'Animal similes' to introduce the activity. Discuss the characteristics of the animals in the similes and what the simile tells you about the person described. Let the children choose similes to devise dialogues around characters with those qualities. Extend by considering the predictability of the simile and ask the children to think of their own comparisons, sharing ideas on other things that are slippery, slow and so on.

Further ideas

● **Adjective collocations:** Can the children suggest nouns that collocate with different adjectives? Prompt them to suggest less obvious examples. For example, *heavy* might prompt responses directly associated with weight, such as *bag*, but could lead to *cold*, *rain*, *traffic* and *sleeper*.

● **More pairs:** Investigate other collocations or binomials, such as those using *or* (*all or nothing* and *rain or shine*). Explore antonyms, synonyms, alliteration and rhyme. Try exploring trinomials (*blood, sweat and tears*, *lock, stock and barrel*), cockney rhyming slang (*apples and pears*, *trouble and strife*) and names (*Jack and Jill*).

● **Similes and clichés:** Use shared reading and writing to collect and use powerful and original similes. Let the children rewrite familiar stories using similes. They could describe themselves or a book character using similes or make up a character, monster or alien to describe.

What's on the CD-ROM

On the CD-ROM you will find:
● Printable versions of all three photocopiable pages.
● Answers to all three photocopiable pages.
● Interactive versions of all three photocopiable pages.

Collocations and similes

Colour collocations

■ We often use colours in phrases. We don't always mean that something is actually that colour. For example, if we say that someone was caught red-handed, we mean that they were caught at the very moment of doing something wrong.

■ Under each colour list the words that make phrases. Use a dictionary to help you find the answers and the meanings of the phrases.

red	white	blue
handed		

handed	elephant	water	lie	blood
flag	herring	feather	letter day	
	murder	carpet	moon	

■ Find words that go with **green** to make phrases.

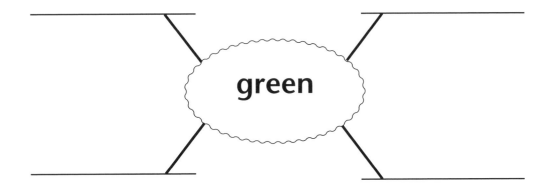

Illustrations © 2010, Woody Fox.

Name:

Collocations and similes

Inseparable pairs

■ Read the poem and underline or highlight the food pairs. The first one has been done for you.

My favourite foods
Bacon and eggs
Bubble and squeak
Then toast and marmalade.
Cheese and onion crisps
Or salt and vinegar
And even chilli and chocolate.
Fish and chips
With salt and vinegar
And bread and butter.
Sweet and sour
Meat and two veg
And steak and kidney pie.

■ Cut out these cards to make pairs. Write them in your book or on a separate sheet of paper with **and** between the pairs.

sugar	law	cops	hide
order	bed	rock	hustle
high	seek	low	breakfast
bustle	robbers	spice	roll

SCHOLASTIC
www.scholastic.co.uk

Illustrations © 2010, Woody Fox.

Collocations and similes

Animal similes

■ When we say something is like something else we are using a simile. Similes contain the words **like** or **as**. They can be used to make our writing more interesting or humorous. Lots of similes compare people to animals.

I was as busy as a bee all morning, packing for my holiday.

My sister dives well and swims like a fish.

■ Choose the right animal from the box to complete the similes.

owl	cats and dogs	eel
pig	bird	tortoise	lamb
mouse	bat	hawk

1. She's as slippery as an _____.

2. He eats like a _____.

3. He's as blind as a _____.

4. She's as wise as an _____.

5. They fought like _____.

6. Grandpa is as slow as a _____.

7. He had eyes like a _____.

8. He's as gentle as a _____.

9. She sings like a _____.

10. You are as quiet as a _____.

Illustrations © 2010, Woody Fox.

Playing with meaning

Objective

To learn that the sounds of some words imitate their meanings.

Background knowledge

Onomatopoeia is when a spoken word sounds like the thing it refers to, such as *bang*, *crash* and *whizz*. It is the only case in English of a word that has a direct connection with the thing it describes. The word *onomatopoeia* combines the Greek words *onoma* (meaning name) and *poieo* (meaning make or do). So an onomatopoeic word names and does what it says. Onomatopoeia is used a lot in poetry, advertisements and comics, as well as for animal noises (*moo*, *tu-whit tu-whoo*). Machine sounds are often described with onomatopoeia (*honk*, *beep-beep*, *vroom*) as well as in science fiction (*zap*).

Activities

These activities explore meaning through sound, using the contexts of school dinnertime, fireworks and bells.

● **Photocopiable page 117 'Dinnertime sounds'**
Start by asking the children to close their eyes for one minute and listen to all the sounds they hear, in the classroom and outside (voices, clocks, cars, breathing). Write their findings on the board and ask the children to suggest onomatopoeic words that describe the sounds, such as *tick* for a clock or *brum* for a car. Use the sounds collected to create sound poems.

● **Photocopiable page 118 'Fireworks onomatopoeia'**
Share the children's experiences of fireworks before focusing on the sights and sounds. Ask them to suggest words to describe the sounds and use the word

onomatopoeia. When the children have collected words, let them use them to write poems or descriptions. As an ICT link, produce multimedia presentations of their writing, with sound effects.

● **Photocopiable page 119 'The sound of bells'**
Read the poem aloud and discuss the onomatopoeia. Check meanings of unfamiliar words. Ask the children to describe the scene to each other and how it makes them feel, noting that the words themselves contribute to the cheerful atmosphere. After sharing their ideas for words, discuss how different bell sounds evoke different feelings. Think about pitch, vibration and duration to help the children get started.

Further ideas

● **More onomatopoeia:** Ask the children to collect onomatopoeic words associated with different places around school, and then extend to other settings (indoor or outdoor, everyday or unfamiliar). This might include onomatopoeic weather words. This can be valuable for story writing, adding atmosphere to settings and events. Look for onomatopoeia in comic strips, and on radio and television.

● **The Bells:** If appropriate, share the rest of this poem with the children. Although it is demanding, the children can appreciate the way the words reflect the changing tones of the bells and the atmosphere of the poem. Explore different bell sounds in music.

 **What's on the CD-ROM**

On the CD-ROM you will find:
● Printable versions of all three photocopiable pages.
● Answers to 'The sound of bells'.

Playing with meaning

Dinnertime sounds

■ Look at this picture of a school hall at dinnertime. At the bottom of the sheet, write a list of at least six things that might make a sound.

■ Next to each item, write a word or words that could represent the sound that it makes. The first one has been done for you.

clock   tick tock

_____ _____

_____ _____

_____ _____

_____ _____

_____ _____

_____ _____

Illustrations © 2010, Woody Fox.

Name:

Fireworks onomatopoeia

■ Onomatopoeia is when a word sounds like the thing it describes. In the shapes under the picture, write down all the onomatopoeic words you can think of to describe the sound of fireworks and bonfires. The first one has been done for you.

Firework and bonfire sounds

whoosh

Illustrations © 2010, Woody Fox.

PHOTOCOPIABLE

Playing with meaning

The sound of bells

■ Read this poem out loud to a partner and listen for the words that sound like bells ringing.

■ Write the words in the shape below and add more of your own.

■ On another piece of paper, draw a scene that includes bells and write some of your words around the picture.

The Bells

Hear the sledges with the bells-
Silver bells!
What a world of merriment their melody foretells!
How they tinkle, tinkle, tinkle,
In the icy air of night!
While the stars that oversprinkle
All the heavens, seem to twinkle
With a crystalline delight;
Keeping time, time, time,
In a sort of Runic rhyme,
To the tintinnabulation that so musically wells
From the bells, bells, bells, bells,
Bells, bells, bells-
From the jingling and the tinkling of the bells.

Edgar Allan Poe

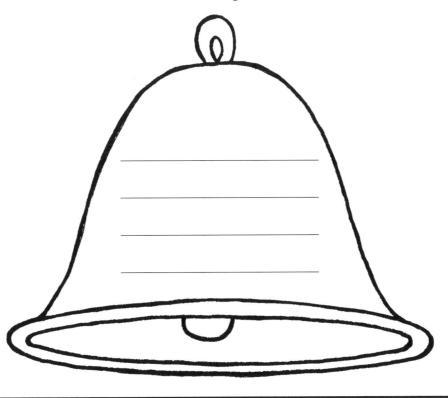

Illustrations © 2010, Woody Fox.

Assessment

Assessment grid

The following grid shows the main objectives and activities covered in this chapter. You can use the grid to locate activities that cover a particular focus that you are keen to monitor.

Objective	Page	Activity title
To learn that signs and symbols sometimes replace words to represent and communicate ideas and meanings.	105 106 107	Washing care symbols Tourism signs Semaphore
To learn to 'read' a range of common signs and symbols.	105 106 107	Washing care symbols Tourism signs Semaphore
To learn that portmanteau words are invented by blending parts of two words to make a new word that combines the sense of both.	109 110 111	Common portmanteau words Inventing words Strange animals
To learn how words are commonly linked together in collocations and similes.	113 114 115	Colour collocations Inseparable pairs Animal similes
To learn that the sounds of some words imitate their meanings.	117 118 119	Dinnertime sounds Fireworks onomatopoeia The sound of bells

Observation and record keeping

Assessment should track the children's development in both knowledge and skills. The children's areas of strength and targets for development might be recorded in the following areas:
● understanding that signs and symbols can communicate meaning and often replace words and that they are simplified images to be 'read' quickly
● knowledge of some common signs and symbols
● understanding that portmanteau words combine words or parts of words to make new words with the combined meanings
● ability to recognise word parts within portmanteau words and work out the meaning of the word
● knowledge that words are often linked together to form common phrases, known as collocations
● developing ability to make writing more interesting by using original phrases and similes
● ability to recognise and generate onomatopoeic words in different contexts.

Assessment activity

● **What you need**
Photocopiable page 121 'Words that go together'.
● **What to do**
The first two parts assess the children's recognition of common collocations. The final activity assesses their ability to generate their own ideas.

Differentiation

● Let less confident learners work orally with an adult who reads the phrase starters aloud. Some may need support to generate ideas for part three.
● Challenge more confident learners to suggest further collocations and similes or to put them into sentences to illustrate use.

Further learning

● **Fostering word consciousness:** Encourage use of adventurous phrases and imagery in writing.
● **Sharing phrases:** Develop a practice of looking for and sharing phrases from shared and personal reading.
● **Dictionaries and thesauruses:** Encourage the children to use dictionaries and thesauruses.

Assessment

Words that go together

■ Collocations are pairs or groups of words that are often found together. Draw lines to match these pairs and then write them underneath with **and** between each pair. The first one has been done for you.

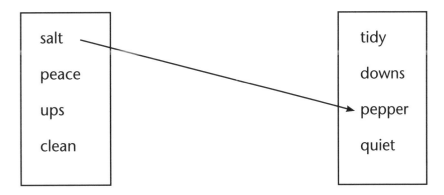

salt and pepper

_____

_____

_____

■ Choose a word from below to complete each simile.

as good as   gold _____

as cold as   _____

as white as   _____

sleep like a   _____

| gold | log | ice | snow |

■ Choose your own words to complete these similes.

as quick as   _____

as slow as   _____

as big as   _____

as small as   _____

Word of the week

The Word of the week pages provide information on one word linked to each section in the chapter. Each word is described in some of the following categories: word definition, word origin, word family, alternative words, fascinating facts and activities. Not all categories are relevant to every word.

You can use the words as a focus to support your work on the different sections of the chapter. For example, you could create a display around it. The information is a starting point for a word focus. The words could form part of your classroom living word bank.

You could also use the word of the week as a springboard to inspire children to think about or research fascinating facts about words, find interesting quotations and to encourage them to use dictionaries and thesauruses.

Sign

- **Word definition:** A noun meaning a gesture, mark or symbol with a meaning. Also a verb meaning to communicate meaning with a mark or gesture.
- **Word origin:** From the Latin *signum*, meaning mark or symbol.
- **Word family:** Verb: *sign*, *resign*, *design*; noun: *signature*, *signal*, *design*, *resignation*, *insignia*; compound word: *signpost*, *sign language*.
- **Alternative words:** Badge, emblem, indicator, label, mark, notice, poster, symbol.
- **Fascinating facts:** The Latin *signum* became *signer* in French, and then *sign* in English, losing its hard /g/ and gaining a long /i/ sounds in the process. Other words in the family, such as *signal*, retain these sounds, which can assist spelling and help the children make meaning connections.
- **Activities:** Find out about signs of the zodiac, Chinese zodiac and sign language.

> Linked section:
> Signs and symbols,
> page 104

Eurovision

- **Word definition:** A noun, referring to the European television network and by extension the Eurovision Song Contest, an annual singing competition among countries in Europe, and one or two others, such as Israel.
- **Word origin:** *Europe* and *vision*. *Europe* from the Greek goddess, Europa. *Vision* from the Latin *videre*, meaning to see.
- **Word family:** Noun: *Europe*, *a European*, *Euro* (currency); adjective: *European*.
- **Fascinating facts:** The Eurovision Song Contest began in 1956 and is one of the longest running television programmes in the world and one of the most-watched non-sporting events, with up to 600 million viewers across the world.
- **Activities:** As a cross-curricular link to geography, find out which countries participated in the last contest and mark these on a map. Find out about the capitals and flags of these countries.

> Linked section:
> New words,
> page 108

(Blue) moon

- **Word definition:** A noun, the moon is a natural satellite of the Earth. *Blue moon* is used metaphorically to describe a rare event, *once in a blue moon*.
- **Word origin:** From the Latin *mensis*, meaning month.
- **Word family:** Adjective: *moonless*; compound word: *moonbeam*, *moonlight*, *moonshine*, *moonstone*, *moonstruck*.
- **Fascinating facts:** *Blue moon* is the name given to a particular full moon that occurs only occasionally. Most years have 12 full moons, roughly once a month, but each calendar year has 12 lunar cycles and a few days extra. The extra days build up so that every two or three years there is an extra full moon, known as a *blue moon*, which means two in one month.
- **Activities:** Find out about lunar (from the Latin *luna*, meaning moon) cycles and other names for moons, such as *new*, *crescent* and *harvest*.

> **Linked section:** Collocations and similes, page 112

Tintinnabulation

- **Word definition:** An abstract noun, meaning a ringing or tinkling sound or bell-ringing.
- **Word origin:** From the Latin *tinnire*, meaning to jingle, with the first syllable repeated.
- **Word family:** Noun: *tintinnabulum* (a high-pitched bell), *tinnitus* (medical condition, constant ringing in the ears); verb: *tintinnabulate*; adjective: *tintinnabular*, *tintinnabulant*.
- **Fascinating facts:** Poe's poem seems to be the best-known record of the word, but it was in use before *The Bells* was published in 1849. Dickens used it in *Dombey and Son* in 1847. *Tintinnabulation* seems to have been a later development from *tintinnabulary*, a bell-ringer, recorded in the 18th century.
- **Activities:** Enjoy the onomatopoeic quality of the word itself. Explore ringing sounds with percussion instruments.

> **Linked section:** Playing with meaning, page 116

Fun with words

Use these activities to support the vocabulary work in this chapter. They could be used as starter or plenary activities.

Symbols
● Invite the children to prepare cards with symbols relating to a particular context, such as international signs or road signs, with meanings on separate cards. Use them to play matching games, pairs, bingo or 'fastest finger first' recognition.

Blanks
● Prepare cards on each of which is a word that a number of other words might be collocated with, followed by a line to represent a blank, such as *beautiful* _____.
In advance, on the back of the card write your own choice of collocation. Give the starter word to the children and ask them each to write down a word that goes with it. For example, for *beautiful* _____ the children might write *weather*, *flower*, *girl*, *dress* and *butterfly*. You then say your answer and the children earn a point if they have written the same word as yours. This works well with adjectives, such as *happy*, *sweet*, *juicy*, *delicious*, *ripe*, *young* and *round*. See www.examples-help.org.uk/parts-of-speech/list-of-adjectives. htm for a comprehensive list of adjectives.

Categories
● Play in pairs or groups. Draw up a list of categories, such as animals, plants, gadgets and sports. Each pair or team picks a different category and writes down a list of things in that category. They then have to make new words by combining words or parts of words. A new sport, for example, might be *rugnis* (a cross between *rugby* and *tennis*). Teams could then write each new word on a card and draw a picture of what it would look like on another. They exchange cards to see if other teams can match words and pictures.

Last man standing
● Choose two children to begin the game. Give them a word that is part of a well-known pair, followed by *and*, such as *salt and…* or *bread and…* The first player to give an appropriate word to complete the pair stays standing and another player joins in. Others can challenge a word if they do not think it makes an appropriate pair with the given word.

Blank similes
● Give parts of similes with blanks, such as *as happy as…* or *as… as spaghetti* and ask the children to write down words or phrases to fill the gaps. Award points for anything suitable and bonuses for particularly interesting choices, inviting the children to vote on certain suggestions.

Rebus puzzles
● Rebus puzzles are word puzzles, for example *ban ana* would be *banana split* or *gegs* would be *scrambled eggs*. They can also use simple line art to illustrate them. They are tricky, but fun. Present words and phrases to suggest meaning in a cryptic way.

Word bank

The word bank comprises ten separate lists of words, two for each chapter. Each list reflects the focus of one section or activity in the chapter. The lists are arranged into three groups: basic, intermediate and advanced. The grouping is not based on the length of a word or its spelling, but on the concepts encompassed by it or the frequency with which it is likely to be encountered in speech or writing. It is expected that most children will understand the meaning of and be able to use the basic vocabulary, that many will use words in the intermediate group, and that the more articulate speakers and confident writers will make the most adventurous choices, reflected in the advanced set.
The words in the lists are not intended as words simply to be learned, either their meanings or their spellings. They are just a sample of the wide range of vocabulary that children should be learning in order to enhance their speaking and writing. Some of the words appear in the related activity itself but many are additional to further extend vocabulary and prompt children's own ideas. Suggested words can be used to support the linked activity or activities directly, but should also be used beyond the activity in a range of contexts, both oral and written, to consolidate meaning. The word lists could be used as a starting point for personal word banks that children can draw on in future spoken and written tasks, or for displays of vocabulary for different contexts.

Adjectives to describe characters   Chapter 1

Basic	Intermediate	Advanced
silly	foolish	irresponsible
lazy	idle	indolent
clever	sensible	shrewd
busy	active	industrious
mean	selfish	miserly
careful	organised	conscientious

Adjectives for mystery story settings

Basic	Intermediate	Advanced
strange	mysterious	inexplicable
dark	gloomy	sombre
scary	eerie	unnerving
dingy	dreary	dismal
creepy	frightening	sinister
spooky	ghostly	unearthly

Prefixes Chapter 2

Basic	Intermediate	Advanced
equal	equate	equation
equidistant	equilateral	equinox
superman	superstar	superpower
superhuman	supersonic	superimpose
hypermarket	hypersonic	hypercritical
hyperactive	hyperlink	hypersensitive

ICT words

Basic	Intermediate	Advanced
mouse	surf	monitor
keyboard	spam	network
screen	virus	software
menu	download	modem
internet	broadband	browser
email	online	megabyte

Adjectives for feelings Chapter 3

Basic	Intermediate	Advanced
sad	miserable	melancholy
happy	contented	radiant
angry	irate	incensed
scared	afraid	petrified
bored	uninterested	jaded
worried	daunted	apprehensive

Conjunctions

Basic	Intermediate	Advanced
and	if	whereas
but	until	although
or	before	yet
so	while	unless
because	after	whether
when	since	whenever

Time words

Basic	Intermediate	Advanced
year	times	age
before	previous	era
after	decade	period
later	century	generation
past	millennium	epoch
ago	reign	lifetime

Describing the effects of weather and other natural phenomena

Basic	Intermediate	Advanced
burning	fiery	searing
freezing	biting	glacial
dry	arid	parched
soaked	drenched	saturated
loud	deafening	thunderous
shaking	heaving	shuddering

Signs and symbols

Basic	Intermediate	Advanced
show	indicate	signify
mean	represent	symbolise
sign	image	insignia
symbol	brand	emblem
mark	logo	cipher
label	icon	motif

Colours

Basic	Intermediate	Advanced
scarlet	crimson	vermilion
navy	azure	aquamarine
lemon	golden	saffron
lime	jade	emerald
mauve	violet	amethyst
tangerine	amber	ochre

Also available in this series:

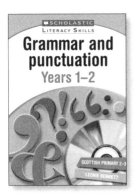
ISBN 978-1407-10045-6

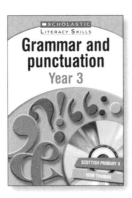
ISBN 978-1407-10046-3

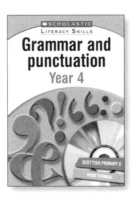
ISBN 978-1407-10047-0

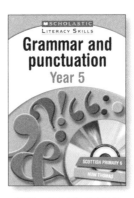
ISBN 978-1407-10048-7

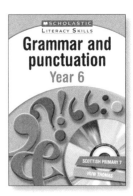
ISBN 978-1407-10049-4

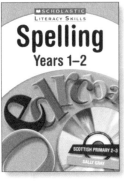
ISBN 978-1407-10055-5

ISBN 978-1407-10056-2

ISBN 978-1407-10057-9

ISBN 978-1407-10058-6

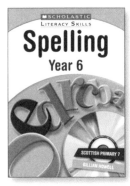
ISBN 978-1407-10059-3

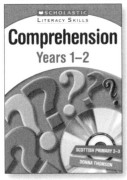
ISBN 978-1407-10050-0

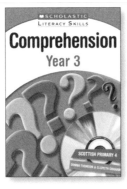
ISBN 978-1407-10051-7

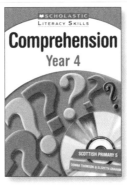
ISBN 978-1407-10052-4

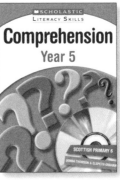
ISBN 978-1407-10053-1

ISBN 978-1407-10054-8

ISBN 978-1407-10223-8

ISBN 978-1407-10224-5

ISBN 978-1407-10225-2

ISBN 978-1407-10226-9

ISBN 978-1407-10227-6

To find out more, call: 0845 603 9091
or visit our website www.scholastic.co.uk